CW00642276

Countering the Cloud

How do cables and data centers think? This book investigates how information infrastructures enact particular forms of knowledge. It juxtaposes the pervasive logics of speed, efficiency, and resilience with more communal and ecological ways of thinking and being, turning technical "solutions" back into open questions about what society wants and what infrastructures should do.

Moving from data centers in Hong Kong to undersea cables in Singapore and server clusters in China, Munn combines rich empirical material with insights drawn from media and cultural studies, sociology, and philosophy. This critical analysis stresses that infrastructures are not just technical but deeply epistemological, privileging some actions and actors while sidelining others.

This innovative exploration of the values and visions at the heart of our technologies will interest students, scholars, and researchers in the areas of communication studies, digital media, technology studies, sociology, philosophy of technology, information studies, and geography.

Luke Munn is a media studies scholar based in Tāmaki Makaurau, Aotearoa New Zealand. His research investigates the sociocultural impacts of digital cultures and their broader intersections with race, politics, and the environment. He is the author of *Unmaking the Algorithm*, *Logic of Feeling*, and *Automation is a Myth*.

Routledge Focus on IT & Society
Series Editor: Harmeet Sawhney, Indiana University, Bloomington

Routledge Focus on IT & Society provides a showcase for cutting-edge scholarship on social aspects of technology and media. This truly interdisciplinary series offers a space for the emergence of offbeat ideas, works from different perspectives that open a window in the mind, methodological agnosticism, flexibility that operates above barriers to interdisciplinary work, and a focus on conceptual payoff of lasting value.

How Information Systems Came to Rule the World
And Other Essays
E. Burton Swanson

Countering the Cloud
Thinking With and Against Data Infrastructures
Luke Munn

Countering the Cloud
Thinking With and Against Data Infrastructures

Luke Munn

Routledge
Taylor & Francis Group

NEW YORK AND LONDON

First published 2023
by Routledge
605 Third Avenue, New York, NY 10158

and by Routledge
4 Park Square, Milton Park, Abingdon, Oxon, OX14 4RN

Routledge is an imprint of the Taylor & Francis Group, an informa business

© 2023 Luke Munn

ISBN: 978-1-032-37415-4 (hbk)
ISBN: 978-1-032-37642-4 (pbk)
ISBN: 978-1-003-34118-5 (ebk)

DOI: 10.4324/9781003341185

Typeset in Times New Roman
by codeMantra

Contents

1 Epistemic Infrastructures

How do cables and data centers think? This book considers how information infrastructures facilitate particular forms of knowledge production and dissemination. It takes seriously the injunction of other scholars to think "from and within infrastructure" (Anand et al. 2018, 13). The "infrastructural turn" has certainly provided a much-needed stress on the materiality that underpins contemporary life. In this framing: "Infrastructures are matter that enable the movement of other matter" (Larkin 2013, 329). While diverse in discipline, ranging from anthropology to geography and sociology, studies born of this turn are often united in their attempt to make visible the invisible, to reveal the hard underlay of stuff beneath seemingly intangible processes and systems. A flurry of research in recent years has seen excellent studies on military infrastructure (Roberts et al. 2012), undersea cables (Starosielski 2015), the layers of the modern city (Graham 2016), electricity networks (French 2017), and the metro system (Fisch 2018), amongst many others.

These analyses often take an excavative approach, beginning at the surface level of a phenomenon, a product, or a service and then drilling down into their material substrate. In contrast, the approach in this book reverses this direction, moving from materiality to epistemology. How does the structuring of matter structure what can be thought? Infrastructures are ways of knowing or even ways-to-know. This means they are in competition with other ways of knowing or not-knowing.[1] Indeed, the key argument here is that infrastructures accomplish a double move—not only advancing a certain epistemic mode but also crowding out competing models of cognition. If studies have shown how these data infrastructures compete with city dwellers for increasingly scarce water (Hogan 2015), compete with citizens for state funding (Brodie 2020), and compete with state legitimacies in offering new modes of governances (Easterling 2016), this book posits that infrastructures also

DOI: 10.4324/9781003341185-1

compete with other epistemologies, advancing particular ways-of-knowing while marginalizing others. This focus on thinking offers a novel dimension for investigation, making a contribution to studies on data centers and wider infrastructures. This material here is based on my contributions to "Data Centres and the Governance of Labour and Territory," a project funded by the Australian Research Council and led by Brett Neilson and Ned Rossiter. Over two years, we focused on data centers, undersea cables, and other information infrastructures at strategic sites in Hong Kong, Singapore, and Sydney. This exploration delved into the hardware, but also the software, standards, labor, and finance poured into these zones. To map these clusters and understand their operations, I drew heavily on the "gray literature" of planning documents, government permits, financial filings, trade publications, and developer specifications. Much of this material was highly technical, focused on bitrates and throughput, redundancy chains, and cooling specifications. Yet as the project anticipated, the social and political impacts of these "merely technical" infrastructures quickly began to emerge.

While this point seems simple, it can readily be overlooked when skimming through industry literature. There is a kind of hard-headed enthusiasm to much of this material, an excitement about the latest hyperscale data center rooted in detailed specifications around square meter footprints and kilowatts drawn down. These infrastructures are larger and more powerful, moving more information at vastly increased speeds. These infrastructures are smarter and more efficient, doing the same thing while using less resources. These infrastructures are able to absorb shocks and recover from them, modeling forms of resilience.

Together these logics—speed, efficiency, resilience—pervade industry discourse, becoming axiomatic principles. It goes without saying that they are worthwhile, productive, something to be pursued for their own sake. In fact, it is remarkable just how smooth this closure is, how unquestioned this triumvirate of speed, efficiency, and resilience has become. Where does this silent force come from, this triumphant indisputability that does not even need to draw attention to itself? This book aims to pry back open these given modes of thinking and being, converting them to open questions. It seeks not to conduct a knee-jerk critique or simplistic debunking of these values, but instead to pause and consider why they have proved ascendant.

Importantly, it examines them not as abstract ideas, but as modes-of-thought that are always performed, carried out by systems and servers that are painstakingly erected, cables and code that are meticulously engineered. Indeed, one of the things that make infrastructures so powerful is that they model their own ideals. They privilege certain logics and then operationalize them. And in this sense, as later chapters will discuss, they both register wider societal values and establish blueprints for how they should be carried out. To surface this performance, I dig into the specificities of cable speeds, examine the affordances of software, and chart the productivity of servers. These technical details, while sometimes arcane, empirically ground the broader argument, demonstrating how these epistemic ideals are operationalized and their impact on the sociocultural milieu around them.

In this introductory chapter, I briefly present the concept of epistemic infrastructures, taking it up in a different way from its original understanding and situating this intervention alongside related work. In Chapter 2, I apply this concept to two infrastructures in Hong Kong: a high-speed cable and a (proposed) hyperscale data center. These examples demonstrate how the material form and function of infrastructure shape the epistemological, privileging particular ways of accessing and understanding the world. These epistemic infrastructures contribute to epistemic hegemonies, or certain dominant modes of thinking and being. And yet other practices of infrastructuring (social, cultural, technical) can be used to challenge and contest this dominance, fostering alternative modes of knowledge.

In the next chapter, I think through efficiency and waste by visualizing and exploring a dataset taken from a server cluster. For cloud providers, efficiency is all-important. And yet data centers are often highly inefficient, burning enormous amounts of energy for power and cooling while having very low server utilization rates, where work is actually being done. By its own standard, this server cluster is inefficient, failing to perfectly orchestrate the different jobs and tasks assigned to it. However, the logic of efficiency may itself be questioned. Efficiency introduces a particular framing, defining a problem, establishing a goal, and offering a compelling road map forward. If efficiency is clarifying, it is also obfuscating, bracketing out alternative ways of understanding these sociotechnical systems. As hyperscale technology companies dominate data centers, often what is becoming more efficient are exploitative operations.

Efficiency should then be challenged, but without falling back to a familiar valorization of inefficiency. In the final chapter, I think through resilience and failure. Data centers have often been framed as indestructible infrastructures that maintain operations while keeping threats at bay. Data centers certainly attempt to reinforce themselves against environmental catastrophes, human intrusions, and the obsolescence that time itself threatens. Yet data centers also illustrate a shift in the concept of resilience from systems theory to ecological understanding. Rather than anticipating and externalizing threats while maintaining an equilibrium, resilient infrastructures internalize them and adapt to changes. Recent moves to "design in" failure and automate healing demonstrate how data centers strive to integrate such resilience. In embodying and enacting this resilience concretely, infrastructures contribute to an imaginary of resilient-thinking that has broadened to become a framework for the governance of life.

Redefining Epistemic Infrastructures

The term "epistemic infrastructures" is associated with a set of tightly related concepts such as epistemic cultures and epistemic practices theorized by Knorr-Cetina (1999; 2008) over the last two decades. These concepts combined practice theory and actor-network-theory to focus on the broader structures that support practices of knowledge production. If epistemic practices are the patterns of action that organize and assemble knowledge, then epistemic infrastructures are "larger formations that connect [epistemic] practices and sites to each other" (Bueger 2015, 8). More concretely, epistemic infrastructures often refer to the libraries, museums, archives, and other institutional forms that "enable individuals and societies to know what they know and to do what they do" (Hedstrom and King 2006, 113).

Drawing on this understanding, Merz (2006, 99) posits that "different epistemic cultures privilege different forms of digital infrastructure." For instance, fields such as theoretical particle physics use technologies like email in a different way than other disciplines. Yet this framing could also imply an array of pre-existing cultures that simply put technical infrastructures to work in the way they desire. In such a vision, knowledge comes prior; technology is merely the tool that allows it to be shared and disseminated in certain ways. This framing can also be found in work on "knowledge infrastructures" (Edwards et al. 2013), which points to the challenges that museums, research institutes, and libraries face in the age of online learning, metadata, and wikis. Such concerns, while important, retain a somewhat conventional perspective, where technologies take prior human knowledge and amplify or undermine it. Against these assumptions, we need to remember that the human inhabits a technical environment, one that exerts significant influence on our ways of knowing—what is known and can be known. In this light, it would be interesting to take Merz's proposition and reverse it. Could we ask instead how digital infrastructures privilege certain epistemic cultures?

In *Thinking Infrastructures* (2019), Kornberger and his co-editors follow this question. Infrastructures are "investments in form" they argue, and these forms "organize thinking and thought and direct action across multiple settings and multiple temporal scales" (1). Yet almost immediately, they contrast thinking infrastructures to the 19th-century infrastructures of road, rail, and wire (1). Compared to those seemingly antiquated technologies, they frame thinking infrastructures as a distinctly 21st-century affair. If thinking infra-structures are "a wide range of phenomena that structure atten-tion, shape decision-making, and guide cognition," the examples of "rankings, ratings, and algorithms" that complete this definition all-too-quickly suggest a certain kind of contemporary digital sys-tem (1). The volume's contributions, from the sharing economy to social media, follow this cue. Granted, this century has certainly been marked by a more intense focus on cognitive labor and infor-mation technologies (Berardi 2010; Moulier-Boutang 2011). Yet the ability to structure attention and guide cognition did not emerge suddenly with the birth of the mainframe or the advent of the inter-net. Indeed, the force Kornberger and colleagues (2019, 2) attribute to a ride-sharing system—one that renders "visible, knowable and thinkable complex patterns of human interaction"—might be said of any number of infrastructures across a much longer span of time. The infrastructural examples in this book, in fact, are contempo-rary not ancient. But rather than being dictated by a focus on the digital and platforms, they assume that any infrastructure, as an investment in a particular kind of form, can be productively under-stood as a way-to-know. An infrastructure does not have to store files or house a database in order to facilitate forms of knowledge while excluding others.

Further developing this concept, we note that infrastructures are often regarded as structures that "give form to knowledge" (Mattern 2020). Infrastructures allow forms of information to be stored, from stone tablets to the stacks of libraries or the platters of a hard drive. But if infrastructures crystallize or materialize knowledge, they also actively influence it. Harold Innis (2007 [1950], 2008 [1951]) may not have explicitly used the term infrastructure, but he recognized that the very materiality of media systems worked to establish certain biases in the ways knowledge was shaped and propagated. Infrastructures are more than an inert storage device or an archived record of what was learned in the past. Infrastructures are performative in the present, generating particular forms of knowledge that are taken up and built upon. As Parikka notes (2011, 66), power/knowledge is circulated through these machines; they are "not only a representation of what happens but an instructional and hence operational tool for executing time-critical processes in technical environments." Infrastructures not only function in a single direction but also as part of a circuit that alters the scope and shape of thought. In structuring, coordinating, and processing, they help determine what can be perceived, interpreted, and reacted to.

For N. Katherine Hayles, these epistemic technologies mean that we should now distinguish between conscious, human-centered thinking and cognition as a "broader term that does not necessarily require consciousness but has the effect of performing complex modeling and other informational tasks" (2014: 201, see also Hayles 2016, 2018). Technical systems establish an intention and carry out purposive activity. These operations are executed at timescales far below the threshold of human consciousness. And these cognitive processes are distributed, taking place in the form of networked ecosystems such as automated trading and the smart home. "Technical devices cognize and interpret all the time," stresses Hayles (2014: 216), and "these interpretations intersect with and very significantly influence the conscious/unconscious interpretations of humans." As technical infrastructures increasingly permeate urban spaces and everyday life, their cognition comes to shape ours.

The concept of "epistemic infrastructure," then, might be taken up in an alternate way to consider how material form shapes the production and dissemination of knowledge. In one sense, this is a question of design. Infrastructures are a result of a specific design vision: they are embedded with particular assumptions, they operate according to a particular logic, and they are planned with particular use cases in mind (Fry 2010; Dunne and Raby 2014). The outcome of these design decisions is a distinct rather than a universal form. And this infrastructural form inherently facilitates certain modes of thought while rendering others inoperable. Of course, establishing a particular infrastructure in a location isn't totalizing. Other forms of thought are not obliterated or rendered impossible. As the last section will discuss, social infrastructures and their alternative epistemologies will certainly persist. Instead it is a matter of considering which kinds of infrastructure are actively supported—drawing capital, land, labor, and so on— and which are pushed to the edge, surviving in the margins. In this sense, decisions about infrastructure intersect with issues of civic life and urban governance (Yigitcanlar et al. 2008; Klinenberg 2018). If an infrastructure "enables or disables particular kinds of action in the city" (Graham and McFarlane 2015, 1), it also enables or disables particular ways of knowing in that space.

Given this observation, we might temporarily anthropomorphize infrastructure to pose a set of simplified questions: How does an infrastructure think? What does it think of? And what cannot be thought through it? To pursue these questions, the next chapter moves from literature to infrastructure, focusing on two key sites in Tseung Kwan O, Hong Kong.

Note

1 "Ways of knowing" here is a less technical alternative to "epistemology" and follows other disciplines that use this phrase to explore what is known, how it is known, and how it influences practices: from indigenous ways of knowing (Cochran 2008) to designerly ways of knowing (Cross 1982) and ways of knowing in nursing (Carper 1978).

References

Anand, Nikhil, Akhil Gupta, and Hannah Appel. 2018. "Temporality, Politics, and the Promise of Infrastructure." In *The Promise of Infrastructure*, edited by Nikhil Anand, Akhil Gupta, and Hannah Appel, 1–38. Durham, NC: Duke University Press.

Berardi, Franco. 2010. "Cognitarian Subjectivation." *E-Flux*, no. 20 (November). https://www.e-flux.com/journal/20/67633/cognitarian-subjectivation/.

Brodie, Patrick. 2020. "Climate Extraction and Supply Chains of Data." *Media, Culture & Society* 42 (7–8): 1–20. https://doi.org/10.1177/0163443720904601.

Bueger, Christian. 2015. "Making Things Known: Epistemic Practices, the United Nations, and the Translation of Piracy." *International Political Sociology* 9 (1): 1–18. https://doi.org/10.1111/ips.12073.

Dunne, Anthony, and Fiona Raby. 2014. *Speculative Everything: Design, Fiction, and Social Dreaming.* Cambridge, MA: MIT Press.

Easterling, Keller. 2016. *Extrastatecraft: The Power of Infrastructure Space.* London: Verso.

Edwards, Paul N., Steven J. Jackson, and Melissa K. Chalmers. 2013. *Knowledge Infrastructures: Intellectual Frameworks and Research Challenges.* Ann Arbor: University of Michigan.

Fisch, Michael. 2018. *An Anthropology of the Machine: Tokyo's Commuter Train Network.* Chicago, IL: The University of Chicago Press.

French, Daniel. 2017. *When They Hid the Fire: A History of Electricity and Invisible Energy in America.* Pittsburgh: University of Pittsburgh Press.

Fry, Tony. 2010. *Design as Politics.* New York: Berg.

Graham, Stephen. 2016. *Vertical: The City from Satellites to Bunkers.* London: Verso Books.

Graham, Stephen, and Colin McFarlane. 2015. "Introduction." In *Infrastructural Lives: Urban Infrastructure in Context*, 1–14. London: Routledge.

Hayles, N. Katherine. 2014. "Cognition Everywhere: The Rise of the Cognitive Nonconscious and the Costs of Consciousness." *New Literary History* 45 (2): 199–220. https://doi.org/10.1353/nlh.2014.0011.

———. 2016. "The Cognitive Nonconscious: Enlarging the Mind of the Humanities." *Critical Inquiry* 42 (4): 783–808. https://doi.org/10.1086/686950.

———. 2018. *Unthought: The Power of the Cognitive Nonconscious.* Chicago, IL: University of Chicago Press.

Hedstrom, Margaret, and John King. 2006. "Epistemic Infrastructure in the Rise of the Knowledge Economy." In *Advancing Knowledge and The Knowledge Economy*, edited by Brian Kahin and Dominique Foray, 113–34. Cambridge: MIT Press. https://doi.org/10.7551/mitpress/1132.003.0013.

Hogan, Mél. 2015. "Data Flows and Water Woes: The Utah Data Center." *Big Data & Society* 2 (2): 205395171559242. https://doi.org/10.1177/2053951715592429.

Innis, Harold Adams. 2007. *Empire and Communications.* Lanham, MD: Rowman & Littlefield.

———. 2008. *The Bias of Communication.* Toronto: University of Toronto Press.

Klinenberg, Eric. 2018. *Palaces for the People: How Social Infrastructure Can Help Fight Inequality, Polarization, and the Decline of Civic Life.* New York: Crown.

Knorr-Cetina, Karin. 1999. *Epistemic Cultures: How the Sciences Make Knowledge.* Cambridge, MA: Harvard University Press.

———. 2008. "Theoretischer Konstruktivismus: Über Die Einnistung von Wissensstrukturen in Soziale Strukturen." In *Theoretische Empirie: Zur Relevanz Qualitativer Forschung*, edited by Herbert Kalthoff, Stefan Hirschauer, and Gesa Lindemann, 35–78. Frankfurt am Main: Suhrkamp Verlag.

Kornberger, Martin, Geoffrey C. Bowker, Julia Elyachar, Andrea Mennicken, Peter Miller, Joanne Randa Nucho, and Neil Pollock, eds. 2019. *Thinking Infrastructures*. Bingley: Emerald Group Publishing.

Larkin, Brian. 2013. "The Politics and Poetics of Infrastructure." *Annual Review of Anthropology* 42: 327–43.

Mattern, Shannon. 2020. "Case Logics: Making Cities, Buildings, Equipment, & Gadgets That Give Form to Knowledge." Presented at the Lectures at Western University, London, Ontario, February 13. http://www.events.westernu.ca/events/fims/2020-02/case-logics-making-cities.html.

Merz, Martina. 2006. "Embedding Digital Infrastructure in Epistemic Culture." In *New Infrastructures for Knowledge Production: Understanding E-Science*, edited by Christine Hine, 99–119. Hershey, Pennsylvania: Information Science Publishing. https://doi.org/10.4018/978-1-59140-717-1.ch005.

Moulier-Boutang, Yann. 2011. *Cognitive Capitalism*. New York: Polity.

Parikka, Jussi. 2011. "Operative Media Archaeology: Wolfgang Ernst's Materialist Media Diagrammatics." *Theory, Culture & Society* 28 (5): 52–74. https://doi.org/10.1177/0263276411411496.

Roberts, Sue, Anna Secor, and Matthew Zook. 2012. "Critical Infrastructure: Mapping the Leaky Plumbing of US Hegemony." *Antipode* 44 (1): 5–9.

Starosielski, Nicole. 2015. *The Undersea Network*. Durham, NC: Duke University Press.

Yigitcanlar, Tan, Kevin O'Connor, and Cara Westerman. 2008. "The Making of Knowledge Cities: Melbourne's Knowledge-Based Urban Development Experience." *Cities* 25 (2): 63–72. https://doi.org/10.1016/j.cities.2008.01.001.

2 Fast and Slow Knowledge

Over the last decade, Tseung Kwan O in Hong Kong has become a key telecommunications nexus in the region and a strategic site for establishing infrastructural presence. One major infrastructural project to emerge in the last several years at Tseung Kwan O has been the TKO Express. The TKO Express is a fiber-optic subsea cable constructed by Superloop and launched in 2017. Tseung Kwan O was already heavily crowded with major international subsea cables. But cable connections between the local stock exchange data center and the business district across the bay were forced to use a circuitous route that traveled through cross-harbor tunnels. This long detour created a delay between the two points, a latency between when a trade was issued at a financial company and when it was received and executed on the stock exchange. For financial services and traders, low latency is absolutely key (Hasbrouck and Saar 2013; Lewis 2014). For this reason, the TKO Express was designed from the beginning to be the shortest possible path between the HKEX Hosting Services Datacenter—the facility that hosts the Hong Kong Stock Exchange—and the Central Business District. As Superloop's director stressed: "That's important for financial institutions which rely on low-latency connectivity... for transactions that can be won or lost in the blink of an eye" (Qiu 2018).

One of the ways to understand infrastructures as particular knowledge producers is to examine the lengths a company will go to deliver a very specific solution—in this case, the low-latency connectivity desired by financial services (Superloop 2016a). Such a challenge is not just real-world detail, but demonstrates the specificity of an infrastructure. They show the immense labor required to erect *this* form and impose *this* vision—along with its particular epistemology—in the face of physical, organizational, and financial hurdles.

DOI: 10.4324/9781003341185-2

Geographically the TKO cable runs from Chai Wan on Hong Kong Island to the Tseung Kwan O Industrial Estate in the New Territories. The shortest and fastest route between these two points is underwater. Indeed, while other cables branch off to nearby junctions or curve in snake-like patterns to reach their destination, one of the remarkable properties of this cable is just how direct it is. By crossing the harbor, TKO could run 3 kilometers rather than the 29 kilometers of the shortest existing route (Rao 2016). However, this body of water is Victoria Harbor, one of the busiest shipping lanes in the world. In addition to maritime traffic, this area is already crisscrossed by a number of existing cables, pipes, and other infrastructural projects (Superloop 2016a). To even be permitted to work in this space, Superloop had to "consult and obtain appropriate approvals from government departments," explained the director (Qiu 2018), "including planning, civil engineering and marine and environment, as well as permission from other telecommunications providers to cross their cables." The project required over 20 permits and official approvals in all, a process that took two years to complete.

Constructing the lowest latency route also created logistical nightmares in the construction phase. One constant danger for undersea cables is ships. Ships may drag their anchor or trawlers may accidentally snag on the cables, ripping them open. In deep water, this is much less likely. Cables are buried under the seabed and typically contain only a light level of protection. However in shallow or busy water, ships become a major threat and fragile fiber-optic cables are surrounded by armored steel wires (Superloop 2016b). In addition, metal sheaths surround the cable, increasing in thickness as water depths decrease.

As cables ascend up the shoreline to their landing point, this danger is further increased. For the vulnerable transition from ocean to land, Superloop constructed a cable duct. This major material intervention "involved drilling below the foundation of an existing seawall and through the bedrock to the breakout point some 250m in the harbor" (Qiu 2018). The duct slants slowly upward, ending as a hole on land, where it is connected to local networks. For the TKO Express, the duct ended 150 meters inland, requiring a large drilling rig to be buried 1.5 meters under the ground in order "to get the correct angle to avoid the seawall, and successfully construct the duct" (Qiu 2018).

Once the duct was constructed, a ship could lay the cable itself. Accompanied by patrol boats to avoid interference, this ship moved slowly across the bay with a sledge burial tool which simultaneously cut a deep trench in the seafloor, laid the cable at the bottom, and covered this trench back up. These details are not just trivia, but demonstrate the intense material transformations required to support the "instant" information and "real-time" transactions of financial trading. Facilitating these forms of knowledge requires ripping up the seafloor, boring through bedrock, and excavating holes in the dirt. The manipulation of matter on a vast scale results in a connection designed specifically to appeal to financial companies. What forms of thought does this infrastructure foster? Certainly financial markets have a particular type of knowledge that is of interest. As De Scheemaekere (2009, 26) notes, the epistemology of modern finance is concerned with making "the subjective a little less prominent and the quantifiable a little more widespread." To pursue this goal, traders and financial companies focus on price tracking, on future probability, and especially on mathematically modeling uncertainty (Clarke 1999; LiPuma and Lee 2004; Stewart 2012; Lee and Martin 2016).

However, here we might return to the question of how infrastructures themselves shape certain epistemic cultures. Putting traders and institutions to one side, we can consider the materiality and operationality of the low-latency cable and the forms of cognition it privileges. If an infrastructure is a way of knowing, what can be "thought" by the TKO Express? The cable is specifically designed to transmit tiny packets of data like bids and price points in a matter of milliseconds. The world is a financial world and the knowledge that matters is knowledge that reaches you before your competitors. In essence, the cable focuses on information that is digital and accelerate-able while bracketing out other forms of knowledge. Writing on high-frequency financial trading, Seyfert notes that some firms enjoy advantages over others because of such infrastructure. "Informational access" Seyfert (2016, 256) suggests, "is not just related to the amount of information and the identity/sameness of information in different milieus, but also to the formatting and the rates of transmission." Seyfert is noting how critical latency and transmission speeds are for trading. Yet perhaps overlooked here is how the "rates of transmission" shape the "identity of information." Only certain types of knowledge can be packaged into a machine-readable form, transmitted along a cable at the speed of light, and then processed by another machine, all in the space of a few milliseconds. A sell order, an option, a current price update—if these are capsules of intelligence, they are highly specialized ones. In this sense, the TKO cable infrastructure only facilitates a very niche form of information. High-speed cables support high-speed thinking, or what we might call "fast knowledge." While tempting, the point here is not to dismiss such fast knowledge. Already there is a rather conservative humanistic strain running across media studies that recoils against this kind of machinic cognition, whether due to its acceleration (Pardo-Guerra 2010) or automation (Stiegler 2016). For these critics, information has become too fast and too complex. The volume and velocity of data supported by cables like the TKO overwhelm the human and its capacities (Rieder and Simon 2017). The resulting technical condition represents an erosion of human agency and a threat to human judgment. In response, humans must claw back control. To take just one example, we could draw on David Golumbia. Writing on high-frequency trading, Golumbia (2015, 397) concludes that this is a sphere where "human beings must retain not just ultimate but thoroughgoing influence, even if the affordances of the technical system might seem to dramatically outpace those of the human one." In this vision, humans must reassert their "real" judgment in the face of this faux-knowledge of correlation and prediction.

Rather than deriding this knowledge as illegitimate, we stress that it is particular. Particular knowledge enables particular action. Depending on which scholar is drawn upon, the rise of financialization varies in its effects, from intensifying inequality (Piketty 2014), to lowering standards of living and the stability of the economy (Tomaskovic-Devey et al. 2015), appropriating our futures (Durand 2017), and fostering more pervasive forms of accumulation and dispossession (Chakravartty and da Silva 2012). This particularity means that infrastructure always carries out a double move. If infrastructure advances a certain form of knowledge, it does not do so in a vacuum, but in relation to other ways of knowing. Investing vast amounts of capital, time, and labor into this kind of infrastructure is a choice. Such resources are inherently limited. And this means that the decision *for* one infrastructure is always a decision *against* alternative infrastructures—whether technical, social, political, and so on—and their attendant epistemic logics.

With this in mind, we might consider the forms of "slow knowledge" that suffer as a result, becoming under-resourced or ignored. In his remarkable essay on slow knowledge (1996: 700), David Orr states that fast knowledge "creates power structures whose function it is to hold at bay alternative paradigms and worldviews." Orr argues that fast knowledge has risen to become hegemonic, edging out other ways of knowing. Fast knowledge is predicated on a number of assumptions. It assumes that knowledge is always measurable, that it should be usable rather than contemplative, and that there is no distinction between information and knowledge (Orr 1996, 699). In a statement that eerily anticipates the devastating fallout of the financial crisis, Orr suggests that systems of fast knowledge create "social traps in which the benefits occur in the near term while the costs are deferred to others at a later time" (1996, 700). Toward the end of the essay, Orr more explicitly contrasts the two different ways of knowing. A selection of these comparisons include (1996, 701):

> Fast knowledge deals with discrete things;
> slow knowledge deals with context, patterns, and connections.
> Fast knowledge is about "competitive edges" and individual and organizational profit;
> slow knowledge is about community prosperity.
> Fast knowledge is mostly linear;
> slow knowledge is complex and ecological.
> Fast knowledge is often regarded as private property;
> slow knowledge is owned by no one.
> Fast knowledge arises from hierarchy and competition;
> slow knowledge is freely shared within a community.

The financial infrastructure of the TKO Express embodies many of these traits: an infrastructure that can be leased by corporate clients in order to gain a competitive edge and achieve individual or organizational profit. In drawing upon financial and organizational capital and facilitating a form of fast knowledge, it simultaneously contributes to a displacement or destruction of slow knowledge, forms of knowing that are more communally and ecologically focused. Tseung Kwan O had a "lack of community 'kaifong' feeling," noted one resident, "we hardly ever saw our neighbors in 10 years. I wouldn't recognize their faces even in the lift" (DeWolf 2020). Of course, as the last section in this chapter will discuss, this doesn't mean that such forms disappear entirely. Tseung Kwan O, notes the same article (DeWolf 2020), shows how "there is always life between the cracks." Instead it is simply to reiterate that infrastructures are powerful epistemic formations, both advancing particular forms of thought and edging out competing ways of knowing. The next section turns to the second epistemic infrastructure in Tseung Kwan O—or more specifically, to the conflict between two competing infrastructural forms.

Battle of Epistemic Infrastructures

This section examines a battle over a plot of land and the different kinds of knowledge supported by different infrastructures. The Tseung Kwan O Industrial Estate, or TKOIE, had been conceived early on as a site for high tech companies. The estate became populated with data centers aligned with Japan (NTT Communications), China (China Mobile, China Unicom, and China Telecom), Australia (Pacnet), the United Kingdom (Global Switch), and the United States (Digital Realty). As the reputation of the space grew and additional undersea cables were connected, the estate rapidly filled up close to capacity. Such spatial constraints matter deeply in Hong Kong, an island where land is very scarce and the government has invested billions on reclaiming land from the sea (Endicott 2001; Heifetz 2017). Indeed Tseung Kwan O itself was largely built on reclaimed land.

Data center operators were put under pressure to find new plots of land for their infrastructures (Mah 2015). One plot of land in the estate had immense potential, but local residents wanted it for other purposes. On September 11 of 2015, the Hong Kong Town Planning Board (abbreviated here as TPB) met. On the agenda was Area 85, a currently vacant parcel of land located in the Industrial Estate but also very close to residents in LOHAS Park. Area 85 was currently designated as GIC, or "government/institution/community," a broad category that would allow it to be used for community facilities in the future. However, the Board had issued a plan to change its designation, allocating it to a data center. One submission to the meeting supported the plan, stating it "would help promote Hong Kong as a knowledge-based society and eliminate unauthorized uses on the site" (TPB 2015, 11). But a number of residents had submitted their own counter claims, and were now present in order to contest this vision.

Over the course of the next few hours, one resident after another arose to express their opposition to the plan. Ms Chee stated that "she did not know that there was no commercial nor market facilities to meet the basic needs of local residents" when she moved to the area six years earlier (19). Frustratingly, there were still none. She recognized the importance of economic needs as well as social needs. But she stressed that "social needs should take precedence as there were already many data centers in TKO. She urged the Board to allocate the proposed data centre site in the area for the development of a government complex to serve local residents" (19).

Next, Ms Fung, another longtime resident of LOHAS Park, spoke. She emphasized that "local residents had been suffering for years due to the lack of basic and essential facilities in the vicinity to meet their daily needs" (20). She noted that there were already 11 data centers in the Industrial Estate. Instead of allocating Area 85 to another data center, she urged the government to use the site "for the development of a government complex with the provision of market, cooked food centre, indoor recreation centre, public car park, post office and library, etc. to meet the demand of local residents" (20).

Mr. Zhang Meixiong followed. He began by complaining that residents were already surrounded by a number of "incompatible land uses" (21). Incompatibility suggests not only that there are deep-seated differences between a data infrastructure and a community infrastructure but also that these differences are irreconcilable. These disparate infrastructures have logics and imperatives that do not overlap with each other. If epistemological orientations constitute a worldview, these infrastructures occupy separate worlds. While they share the same space of Tseung Kwan O, these differences cannot be smoothed over, cannot be brought into harmony. Meixiong stressed that the allocation of Area 85 was not just an abstract or economic decision, but one fundamental to the lives of its nearby inhabitants (22). Due to the lack of basic needs over so many years, a climate of hostility had emerged in the local community. He concluded by issuing a warning (23), stating that "the strong sentiments of local residents against the Government might be further increased. They might be prone to carry out demonstrations or even violent actions."

Christine Fong, a representative for many residents, then spoke. She reminded the Board that "the proposed data centre sites were the only two vacant sites in the vicinity of LOHAS Park in the area" (25). She argued that "pro-government DC Members, who indicated support to the data centre development... had no local knowledge on the strategic importance of the sites for local residents" (26). Fong's phrasing of "strategic importance" suggests that particular sites—and the infrastructure that attends them—are not only critical for commercial interests like the data center operators, but can also be key for the community. A community center would be an infrastructure that would allow residents to generate their own forms of knowledge, to collectively develop a sense of community identity, and to share that thinking with others.

After hearing all these arguments, the Board adjourned to consider their merit. However, upon returning from deliberations, the Board announced that it had decided "*not* to uphold R2 to R385" [the 384 representations from Residents] and that "the Plan should *not* be amended to meet the representations" (52, emphasis in original). While "sympathetic" to the needs of the community, the board assured them that more facilities would be built for them eventually. Besides, no other alternative sites for data centers had been located. The plan would go ahead. Rather than a community center, Area 85 would become a data center.

The debate over Area 85 presents a clear conflict. Two opposing forces struggle over a single parcel of land and its future function: data center or community center. As in the case of the TKO Express, the decision for the former should be understood as a decision against the latter. Tseung Kwan O is an environment of finite resources: electricity, water, capital, and most critically in Hong Kong—land. This means that the decision takes place with a zero-sum terrain, giving to some while taking away from others. By obtaining Area 85, data center operators will enjoy a designated site, close to a metropolis and low-latency cable links, while residents must make do without their own "epistemic infrastructures"—core community facilities such as a library, a post office, or a market. Admittedly, this example is somewhat unusual in its stark binary. Yet if the battle lines are typically less obvious, they demonstrate a fundamental conflict between different infrastructures and the different forms of epistemologies they facilitate. In framing the Board's decision as one considering "economic" versus "social" concerns, the residents demonstrated their inherent understanding of this tension.

In 2018, the plot went to auction. As Hong Kong's largest parcel of land now zoned for data centers, it was fiercely contested, fetching nine bids from major operators (Ka-sing 2018). In the end, the auction was won by SUNeVision Holdings with a bid 45% higher than the expected price (Zhou 2018). While a new facility has yet to be completed, it is not difficult to envision because SUNeVision already owns the adjacent plot. This facility is the home of premium data center provider Equinix (2019), whose blue-chip clients include cloud computing firms like Amazon Web Services, Google Cloud, and Microsoft Azure and financial firms such as NASDAQ, Paypal, and Lloyds.

If financial firms facilitate forms of knowledge predicated on quantification and monetization, cloud providers produce knowledge through the capture and commodification of social knowledge

(Terranova 2018). As Morozov (2014, 2015, 2018) has long argued, these companies accrue wealth through the extraction of personal data, a highly valuable asset that should be a social rather than a commercial resource. Corporations like Amazon and Google mine this knowledge, folding it into proprietary systems that amplify their reach and increase their competitive advantage. And these providers rely heavily on the kind of highly priced, massively scaled infrastructure that Equinix offers in its TKOIE facility. This is what Andrejevic (2014) calls "the big data divide"—big data exacerbates the power asymmetry between those who have the capital and infrastructure to use it and those who do not, between those who sort and those who are sorted. The epistemic hegemonies of big tech companies emerge from the epistemic infrastructures they are built upon.

This is not just about market dominance, but a kind of outsized cognitive dominance. In this sense, the Californian ideology (Barbrook and Cameron 1995) is also an epistemology, embedded with a certain way of understanding the world. These platforms and services dictate how information should be prioritized, what relations should be enabled, and what actions can be taken. For Leetaru (2019): "Silicon Valley's enforcement of a single set of global rules of what is permissible to say, see, and believe online represents a new generation of enforced cultural colonialism." While Leetaru's claims may be slightly overwrought, they stress how such tech titans go beyond merely being "technology companies" and enact a dominant mode of experiencing the everyday (Greenfield 2017). With user bases in the millions, product and platform paradigms rapidly become normalized.

What epistemologies emerge from this infrastructure of multinational corporations and hyperscale data center facilities? In other words, what forms of cognition are enabled (and disabled) by this intersection of elements? Here we might briefly focus on the burgeoning role of big data and machine learning carried out in these facilities. Frické (2015, 655) carefully deconstructs several of the key techniques used in this area, concluding that "connectionism, neural nets, random forests, and so on in machine learning are, at heart, a black box instrumentalist version of inductive algorithms." These, in turn, are updated versions of inductivism, that long-discredited belief that data alone will provide theories, guide experiments, and provide rich insights. "Who knows why people do what they do? The point is they do it," asserted *Wired* editor Anderson (2008), summing up this epistemology, "with enough data, the numbers speak for themselves." Hypotheses can be discarded; curve-fitting and correlation is all that matters. In this world, relations can be distilled into node values and data provides a ground truth. There is a kind of pragmatism here, an operationalization of life. The style of reasoning employed by algorithmic systems and big data is essentially reductionist, critiques Krasmann (2020), a "logic of the surface." And this is not even to delve into how such data is often biased and racialized, emerging as it does from the substrate of colonial systems (Chun 2018; Benjamin 2019).

Contesting Epistemic Hegemonies

Despite all these critiques, the point is not to dismiss this mode of cognition altogether, but to stress its specificity. In presenting a compelling technocratic worldview, this epistemology brackets out other ways of knowing. The town planning board rationalized a data center by stating it would facilitate a "knowledge-based society." But what kinds of knowledge are included and excluded in this vision? Here, as the chapter has stressed, it pays to attend to the affordances of infrastructures. The epistemic infrastructures of the high-speed cable and the hyperscale data center are designed in a particular way. These designs are not infinitely open-ended. In contrast to some of the earlier framings of epistemic infrastructures, infrastructures cannot simply be taken up by various cultures to produce whatever forms of knowledge are desired. There is a relation between operation and cognition, between what can be done and what can be known.

On the one hand, there are certain hard limits imposed by functionality: some operations are impossible. A data center, for instance, cannot store, process, or redistribute information that is non-digital. This immediately ignores a vast realm of knowledge that is irreducible to bytes, precluding, for instance, key aspects of indigenous knowledge systems. As Charles Kamau Maina (2012, 17) stresses, digital information management "excludes traditional knowledge that is not formerly codified and is acquired not through research but through, *inter alia*, inspiration and life experiences." These are epistemologies that are not fully expressible in the terms of capture (Agre 1994), ways of knowing that are not easily ingested, parsed, and processed. Some knowledge systems do not conform to the matrix-like logic of the digital, with its classifications and codes. The question here is what is ignored, what is incompatible, what remains outside the epistemic frame? The framing function of an epistemic infrastructure is powerful precisely because it banishes this question and quietly sets out the boundaries of what can be known.

On the other hand, there is a softer shaping of knowledge that infrastructures carry out. Some forms of knowledge generation are technically achievable, but are discouraged in favor of other uses. In theory, the high-speed cable could transmit many kinds of information. In practice, the cable's tight design specifications (and the exorbitant costs associated with renting access to it) mean that it remains the domain of elite financial firms and high-speed trading data. This is an infrastructure for fast knowledge—even if others were granted free access to the cable, the transmission of alternative forms of knowledge (slower, more communal, less commercial) would be considered cross-purpose, out of place, a "waste" of its capabilities. What then are the modes of cognition that are privileged by an infrastructure, the processes they are optimized for and through which knowledge is considered to emerge? Machine learning and big data, touched on above, often come with a strong set of epistemic assumptions, a particular understanding of the world linked with a claim to be an "all-knowing prognosticator or a shortcut to ground truth" (Crawford et al. 2014, 1670). In structuring matter, infrastructures also structure thought, reinforcing established ways of thinking while marginalizing others.

Of course, this is not to claim that alternative forms of knowledge disappear. Lighting up a high-speed cable does not suddenly erase non-financial knowledge. Similarly, launching a data center does not delete more social and communal forms of knowing. Despite Kittler's warning (1999: xxxix), media do not entirely determine our situation, nor do infrastructures completely dictate knowledge. Systems are never totalizing and alternative forms of thought continue outside formal systems. "While infrastructure sets lines of articulation and instantiates particular conceptions of space and time," stresses AbdouMaliq Simone (2015, 120), "it always engenders shadows, recesses, and occlusions that can be occupied as staging areas for unscripted incursions." Knowledge may take place at the peripheries of the formal economy like the market. And the transmission of this knowledge may employ more ad-hoc forms of exchange such as the story or the joke. Within this "relational infrastructure," Simone (2015, 84) suggests that the "marginalized, weakened or threatened" work out their own "operational spaces"—however temporary. If cloud platforms, with their megawatts of electricity and millions of dollars of capital, represent a kind of high-power knowledge generation system, the conversation between locals at a street-side stall embodies its low-power opposite.

One recent counter-infrastructure in the city has been driven by Hong Kong's anti-extradition protests. From the city center to Tseung Kwan O itself, these protests have seen millions take to the streets, coordinated actions that were supported by a sophisticated social-digital infrastructure. Groups have been setup on encrypted messaging apps and online forums, some with tens of thousands of participants. These groups have facilitated a rich form of crowd-sourced knowledge used to organize marches, share legal and medical advice, warn others of police, and offer supplies like masks, while real-time voting on the same groups allows this leaderless movement to debate the use of violence or the location of the next action (Vincent 2019). These examples are not just about a "clever use" of digital tools, but can be understood as an epistemic infrastructure, constructed from the ground up, which aims to think about Hong Kong in a fundamentally different and more democratic way. Though opinion certainly varies across the movement, this alternative knowledge formation coalesces around the idea that Hong Kong is not just a data-driven financial powerhouse (Lewis et al. 2019; Yiu 2019; Ellis 2020), nor an extension of China, but a space with its own values and visions. Far from technophobic, this infrastructure draws upon the very same low-latency cables and hyperscale data centers discussed in the sections above, yet employs these affordances in order to scaffold very different forms of knowledge. This is an immanent intervention, where radical ways of knowing piggyback on established infrastructures while undermining established epistemologies.

Yet while alternative forms of knowledge certainly persist, the force of infrastructure should once more be stressed. The essential question here is what forms of knowing are being actively supported. Infrastructures draw upon vast amounts of capital, labor, and time, mobilizing these limited key resources into a particular form. Once constructed, they intensify and extend particular ways of knowing. In the case of the cable, we might expect to see not only increasing volumes of trades but also new firms being enticed to the city and new forms of financialization being developed. In the case of the data center, we could anticipate an influx of cloud companies and platforms, where more articulated and invasive forms of extraction become operable at scale. These infrastructures amplify dominant modes of thought while undermining alternatives. While social or relational infrastructures will certainly persist in the margins, regardless of being under-resourced, such precarity reduces their potential for greater impact—more stable lives and livelihoods, stronger and more resilient communities, richer forms of cultural and social life. Epistemic infrastructures promote and power epistemic hegemonies.

Rather than simply giving form to knowledge, infrastructures actively shape the production of knowledge. Infrastructures are designed and developed, representing an investment in a particular kind of form. In connecting particular institutions, producing particular forms of information, and distributing them at particular temporalities, this infrastructural form apprehends and understands the world in a particular way. Epistemic infrastructure always enacts a double move—funneling land, labor, and capital into a form which fosters a certain kind of knowledge while suppressing or ignoring alternative ways of knowing. Certainly, infrastructures are not totalizing. Alternative epistemologies—slower, more local, more communal—continue to persist. However, we should also recognize the ability of epistemic infrastructures to engender forms of epistemic hegemony. As social infrastructures become more neglected, dominant infrastructures grow in scale and reach, fostering extractive forms of knowledge-production and normalizing "universal" and commercial ways of thinking. Reframing infrastructures as epistemic stresses that infrastructures are not merely complex technical systems, but at a far more fundamental level, ways to know. Resituating them in this way moves them away from being the sole domain of technologists and experts, and places them in the wider hands of communities and citizens. It stresses the everyday stakes of infrastructure as a form through which we interpret the world around us. And it poses a more accessible but more profound set of questions: what do we want to know and how do we want to think?

References

Agre, Philip E. 1994. "Surveillance and Capture: Two Models of Privacy." *The Information Society* 10 (2): 101–27.

Anderson, Chris. 2008. "The End of Theory: The Data Deluge Makes the Scientific Method Obsolete." *Wired*, June 23, 2008. https://www.wired.com/2008/06/pb-theory/.

Andrejevic, Mark. 2014. "The Big Data Divide." *International Journal of Communication* 8: 1673–89.

Barbrook, Richard, and Andy Cameron. 1995. "The Californian Ideology." *Metamute* 1 (3). https://www.metamute.org/editorial/articles/californian-ideology.

Benjamin, Ruha. 2019. *Race After Technology: Abolitionist Tools for the New Jim Code.* London: Polity.

Chakravartty, Paula, and Denise Ferreira da Silva. 2012. "Accumulation, Dispossession, and Debt: The Racial Logic of Global Capitalism-An Introduction." *American Quarterly; College Park* 64 (3): 361–85.

Chun, Wendy Hui Kyong. 2018. "Critical Data Studies or How to Desegregate Networks." *Presented at the CHCI 2018,* Charlottesville, VA, July 31. https://www.youtube.com/watch?v=Qhp80UXTvaQ.

Clark, Malcolm. 1999. *The Midas Formula: Trillion Dollar Debt.* BBC Horizon. http://documentaryvine.com/video/midas-formula-trillion-dollar-bet/.

Crawford, Kate, Mary L. Gray, and Kate Miltner. 2014. "Critiquing Big Data: Politics, Ethics, Epistemology." *International Journal of Communication* 8: 1663–72.

De Scheemaekere, Xavier. 2009. "The Epistemology of Modern Finance." *Journal of Philosophical Economics* 2 (2): 99–120.

DeWolf, Christopher. 2020. "Once Hong Kong's 'Little Taiwan', Tseung Kwan O Has a Rich History, Hidden Qualities – but Is It Still a Little Bland?" *South China Morning Post,* February 24, 2020. https://www.scmp.com/lifestyle/travel-leisure/article/3051552/once-hong-kongs-little-taiwan-tseung-kwan-o-has-rich.

Durand, Cédric. 2017. *Fictitious Capital: How Finance Is Appropriating Our Future.* London: Verso.

Ellis, Eric. 2020. "Can Hong Kong Endure as a Financial Centre?" *Euromoney,* January 13, 2020. https://www.euromoney.com/article/bljsr3gxwl8wvf/can-hong-kong-endure-as-a-financial-centre.

Endicott, L. J. 2001. "Drained Reclamation in Hong Kong." In *Soft Soil Engineering,* edited by A. K. L. Kwong. Lisse, the Netherlands: Svets and Zeitlinger.

Equinix. 2019. "SEC Filing." Securities and Exchange Commission. February 22, 2019. http://investor.equinix.com/node/25691/html.

Frické, Martin. 2015. "Big Data and Its Epistemology." *Journal of the Association for Information Science and Technology* 66 (4): 651–61. https://doi.org/10.1002/asi.23212.

Golumbia, David. 2015. "Judging like a Machine." In *Postdigital Aesthetics,* edited by David Berry and Michael Dieter, 123–35. New York: Springer.

Greenfield, Adam. 2017. *Radical Technologies: The Design of Everyday Life.* London: Verso.

Hasbrouck, Joel, and Gideon Saar. 2013. "Low-Latency Trading." *Journal of Financial Markets* 16 (4): 646–79. https://doi.org/10.1016/j.finmar.2013.05.003.

Heifetz, Justin. 2017. "Hong Kong's Government Is Spending Billions Taking Land from the Sea." *Vice* (blog). November 10, 2017. https://

www.vice.com/en_us/article/wjgpm9/hong-kong-spending-billions-taking-land-from-sea.

Ka-sing, Lam. 2018. "Hong Kong's Biggest Data Centre Plot Fetches Nine Bids." *South China Morning Post*, December 7, 2018. https://www.scmp.com/property/hong-kong-china/article/2176955/hong-kongs-biggest-and-last-data-centre-plot-fetches-nine.

Kittler, Friedrich. 1999. *Gramophone, Film, Typewriter.* Stanford, CA: Stanford University Press.

Krasmann, Susanne. 2020. "The Logic of the Surface: On the Epistemology of Algorithms in Times of Big Data." *Information, Communication & Society* Ahead-of-print (February): 1–14.

Lee, Benjamin, and Randy Martin, eds. 2016. *Derivatives and the Wealth of Societies.* Chicago, IL: University of Chicago Press.

Leetaru, Kalev. 2019. "Is A Fragmented Internet Inevitable?" *Forbes*, April 13, 2019. https://www.forbes.com/sites/kalevleetaru/2019/04/13/is-a-fragmented-internet-inevitable/#74acd692223c.

Lewis, Leo, Don Weinland, and George Hammond. 2019. "Doubts Grow over Hong Kong's Future as Financial Centre amid Protests." *Financial Times*, November 28, 2019. https://www.ft.com/content/05151ff2-1113-11ea-a7e6-62bf4f9e548a.

Lewis, Michael. 2014. *Flash Boys: A Wall Street Revolt.* New York: W. W. Norton & Company.

LiPuma, Edward, and Benjamin Lee. 2004. *Financial Derivatives and the Globalization of Risk.* Durham, NC: Duke University Press.

Mah, Paul. 2015. "Hong Kong's Data Center Hub Is Pushed for Space." April 21, 2015. https://www.datacenterdynamics.com/en/news/hong-kongs-data-center-hub-is-pushed-for-space/.

Maina, Charles Kamau. 2012. "Traditional Knowledge Management and Preservation: Intersections with Library and Information Science." *The International Information & Library Review* 44 (1): 13–27. https://doi.org/10.1016/j.iilr.2012.01.004.

Morozov, Evgeny. 2014. "How Much for Your Data?" *Le Monde Diplomatique*, August 1, 2014. https://mondediplo.com/2014/08/07data.

———. 2015. "Socialize the Data Centres!" *New Left Review*, II, no. 91: 45–66.

———. 2018. "After the Facebook Scandal It's Time to Base the Digital Economy on Public v Private Ownership of Data." *The Observer*, March 31, 2018, sec. Technology. https://www.theguardian.com/technology/2018/mar/31/big-data-lie-exposed-simply-blaming-facebook-wont-fix-reclaim-private-information.

Orr, David W. 1996. "Slow Knowledge." *Conservation Biology* 10 (3): 699–702.

Pardo-Guerra, Juan Pablo, Daniel Beunza, Yuval Millo, and Donald Mackenzie. 2010. *Impersonal Efficiency and the Dangers of a Fully Automated Securities Exchange.* London: Foresight. http://eprints.lse.ac.uk/43589/1/Impersonal%20efficiency%20and%20the%20dangers%20of%20a%20fully%20automated%20securities%20exchange%20author%20%28LSERO%29.pdf.

Piketty, Thomas. 2014. *Capital in the Twenty First Century*. Translated by Arthur Goldhammer. Cambridge, MA: Belknap Press.

Qiu, Winston. 2018. "Inside Story of TKO Express Construction." *Submarine Networks*. June 24, 2018. https://www.submarinenetworks.com/en/ systems/intra-asia/tko-express/inside-story-of-tko-express-construction.

Rao, Pranav. 2016. "Superloop Investor Presentation." Investor Relations, Singapore, September 14. https://www.slideshare.net/PranavRao17/ superloop-investor-presentation.

Rieder, Gernot, and Judith Simon. 2017. "Big Data: A New Empiricism and its Epistemic and Socio-Political Consequences." In *Berechenbarkeit der Welt? Philosophie und Wissenschaft im Zeitalter von Big Data*, eited by Wolfgang Pietsch, Jörg Wernecke, and Maximilian Ott, 85–105. Wiesbaden: Springer Fachmedien. https://doi. org/10.1007/978-3-658-12153-2_4.

Seyfert, Robert. 2016. "Bugs, Predations or Manipulations? Incompatible Epistemic Regimes of High-Frequency Trading." *Economy and Society* 45 (2): 251–77. https://doi.org/10.1080/03085147.2016.1213978.

Simone, AbdouMaliq. 2015. "Relational Infrastructures in Postcolonial Urban Worlds." In *Infrastructural Lives: Urban Infrastructure in Context*, edited by Stephen Graham and Colin McFarlane. London: Routledge.

Stewart, Ian. 2012. "The Mathematical Equation That Caused the Banks to Crash." *The Observer*, February 12, 2012, sec. Science. http:// www.theguardian.com/science/2012/feb/12/black-scholes-equation-credit-crunch.

Stiegler, Bernard. 2016. *Automatic Society*. Cambridge: Polity Press.

Superloop. 2016a. "TKO Express, Why?" *TKO Express* (blog). November 30, 2016. http://tkoexpress.com/tko-express-why/.

——. 2016b. "TKO Express» Twice the Protection." *TKO Express* (blog). December 14, 2016. http://tkoexpress.com/twice-the-protection/.

Terranova, T. 2018. "Data Mining the Body of the Socius." Staatliche Museen Zu Berlin. 2018. https://smart.smb.museum/export/downloadPM. php?id=5349.

Tomaskovic-Devey, Donald, Ken-Hou Lin, and Nathan Meyers. 2015. "Did Financialization Reduce Economic Growth?" *Socio-Economic Review* 13 (3): 525–48. https://doi.org/10.1093/ser/mwv009.

Town Planning Board. 2015. "Minutes of 1093rd Meeting." https://www. info.gov.hk/tpb/en/meetings/TPB/Minutes/m1093tpb_e.pdf.

Vincent, Danny. 2019. "How Apps Power Hong Kong's Leaderless Protests." *BBC News*, June 30, 2019. https://www.bbc.com/news/technology-48802125.

Yiu, Enoch. 2019. "Hong Kong Shuts Record Number of Banks as Protests Paralyse City." *South China Morning Post*, November 13, 2019. https://www.scmp.com/business/banking-finance/article/3037523/ protest-chaos-leads-most-bank-branch-closings-hong-kongs.

Zhou, Emma. 2018. "SHK's SUNeVision Wins Bid for Hong Kong Data Centre Site." *Mingtiandi*. December 15, 2018. https://www.mingtiandi. com/real-estate/projects-real-estate/shks-sunevision-wins-bid-for-hong-kong-data-centre-site/.

3   Efficiency and Waste

Uber, Airbnb, Google, Amazon, and Netflix are names that stress how data-driven systems are reshaping the world. Yet these platforms and services would not be possible without the data infrastructure that underpins them. Far from being nebulous and immaterial, "the cloud" is highly material, taking the form of the copper and cables, switches and server racks that comprise the data center and its accompanying infrastructure (Holt and Vonderau 2015). Often overlooked by consumers, these data centers nevertheless play a critical role, delivering media streams, ferrying financial transactions, storing health data, and deriving insights through machine learning. As everyday activities increasingly become digitally mediated, the control and distribution of this data becomes not just a technical question, but a social and political one (Ruppert et al. 2017).

Yet if data centers are increasingly influential, they are often conceived as black-boxes (Pinch 1992; Veel 2017). Typically off limits to researchers, what can be determined is often gleaned from high-level technical specifications: a building spanning several thousand meters of floor space, which may contain a certain number of server racks, and which is driven by an infrastructure capable of producing a certain amount of power. Specific details—the names and numbers of clients, the precise amount of water and energy used, the routing of data, and the largest markets—are all proprietary information that remains undisclosed for reasons of both client security and business competitiveness.

Recently however, Alibaba, the Chinese cloud computing giant, released major datasets from its production cluster (Alibaba 2019). In essence, a production cluster is simply a large number of servers that are grouped together by scheduling software. The cluster management system assigns jobs to machines in the cluster and manages the allocation of resources to it. The 2017 dataset includes

DOI: 10.4324/9781003341185-3

about 1,300 machines over a period of 12 hours. The 2018 dataset is much larger and more detailed, with five files totaling 270 giga-bytes, and includes data from around 4,000 machines over a period of eight days.

Certainly there are limitations in this dataset. Unfortunately, Alibaba does not disclose exactly where this cluster is located, nor whether these machines are housed in a single data center or spread across multiple sites. Moreover, while the times and dura-tions of jobs are given, what exactly the job entails—Moving data? Performing queries on databases? Generating machine learning models?—is never specified. Finally, machines are simply num-bered as a series—how they are racked or arranged spatially in the building is unknown. As with any dataset, these gaps set limits on what can be inferred. However, given the typically black-boxed nature of data centers, the public release of this information does offer an interesting resource for researchers and a welcome step to-ward transparency from cloud operators.

Why was this data made publicly available? To a certain extent, Alibaba's claim that they are helping to "bridge the knowledge gap between many of us and academic researchers/industrial experts" is not unfounded (Alibaba Developer 2019). Without voluntary re-lease of this information, it would be off limits to all but a handful of data center employees. However, the publishing of this data is not entirely selfless. At the time of writing, eight journal articles had been produced based on this dataset (Lu et al. 2017; Cheng et al. 2018; Jiang et al. 2019; and others). Alibaba links to these ar-ticles from the cluster webpage and encourages authors to notify them when an article is published. Each article analyses the data in different ways and delivers its own findings in terms of problems and possible improvements. As one paper observes: "researchers can study the workload characteristics, analyze the cluster status, design new algorithms to assign workloads, and help to optimize the scheduling strategies between online services and batch jobs for improving throughput while maintaining acceptable service quality" (Ren et al. 2018, 2). By releasing the data, Alibaba gets to draw on the expertise and training of dozens of computer scientists around the world. Their knowledge production provides valuable insights, which in turn may become folded back into day-to-day operations at the cloud company.

In this chapter, the Alibaba archive is explored through data vi-sualization. Of course, data visualization itself is subjective rather than objective (Jurgenson et al. 1995). While it provides a way of understanding information, it is a mediation rather than a direct translation, a method that reveals some things while obscuring others. Decisions made by the designer concerning parameters, color, and form influence what is seen by the viewer (Kosara 2008). Nevertheless, these depictions can provide a productive way of exploring data and communicating dynamics in a visual rather than textual form. Data visualization can be particularly helpful in presenting essential information in big data (Keim et al. 2013). Data visualization can draw out trends or relationships from the millions of data points in these vast repositories, which can often seem arbitrary or formless. If these patterns are made clear by design, they are beneficial in initiating a broader discussion.

What are the aims of the present work and its broader intervention? Certainly exploring the normally inaccessible operations of a real-world data center is of interest. Yet the intent here is not to improve data center efficiency by delivering a list of optimizations to be implemented. Indeed, the kind of quantitative performance testing carried out in computer science is a highly technical undertaking requiring an engineering background. At the same time, this intervention doesn't want to simply dismiss the notion of efficiency altogether, as might be the tendency when coming from a humanities or social science perspective.

Instead, the chapter uses data center infrastructures as a way to consider efficiency at both an operational and political level. In the first half of the chapter, I explore the complexity and contingency that pervades the data center on a practical level, showing how, even on its own terms, these infrastructures fail to achieve the efficiency ideal. In the last half of the chapter, I move into a discussion that questions efficiency itself and the values, assumptions, and norms bound up with this ideal. In balancing these twin goals, the chapter wants to model a contribution that is technically aware yet also theoretically critical. Such an interdisciplinary approach seems increasingly apt for our contemporary moment where data infrastructures have become a site of significant political force (Rossiter 2017, Ruppert et al. 2017).

This chapter, to briefly signpost, consists of four sections. The first section establishes some context around efficiency in computing and traces a brief history of the struggle to improve it. The second section steps through each data visualization, detailing the ways in which the data center fails to achieve the efficiency imaginary. The third section touches briefly on the industry's scapegoat for this inefficiency: human labor and incomplete automation.

And the fourth section opens out to an extended discussion that questions efficiency more fundamentally. What does this framing device reveal, what does it obscure, and how might we critically understand efficiency within these machine-centric environments?

The Struggle for Efficiency

We begin by examining the data center industry according to efficiency's own terms. Seen through this particular lens, the industry has long struggled. Data centers consume vast amounts of energy in order to power and cool servers, which run around the clock without interruption. Indeed, the voracious appetite of data centers for energy is not slowing. One study estimated (Andrae and Edler 2015) that data centers will use around 3–13% of global electricity in 2030 compared to 1% in 2010. Along with the obvious financial cost, the enormous environmental impact of this demand has increasingly been recognized, even within the industry itself. Papers have begun to analyze and quantify the sustainability of data centers (Marwah et al. 2010). A more recent paper by computer science engineers (Uddin et al. 2015) admitted bluntly: "Data centers are key contributors of greenhouse gas emissions that pollute the environment and cause global warming."

One of the reasons for this inefficiency is that availability is all-important in the industry. Servers must be always-on and always-running, allowing files to be accessed, services to remain online, transactions to complete, and queries to be returned. Quality-of-service contracts between data center operators and clients guarantee extremely high availability rates. "Three nines" (99.9%) availability, once the gold standard, has been ratcheted up in recent years to four, five, or even six nines (Hatzenbuehler 2018). Indeed, a coveted Tier IV rating—an enormously influential metric in the industry—is awarded only to those facilities which can expect a maximum of 20 minutes downtime per year based on their highly redundant infrastructure (Uptime Institute 2018). Interruptions, whether caused by human error or natural disaster, must be avoided at all costs. Yet servers, while constantly draining energy, only spend a fraction of their time and resources carrying out work for clients. "Such low efficiencies," admitted one industry insider, "made sense only in the obscure logic of digital infrastructure" (Glanz 2012).

One of the first widely adopted technologies for improving efficiency was the hypervisor. Gaining its name from being "the supervisor of the supervisor," hypervisors were actually created in the mid-1960s by IBM in order to test different "virtual machines" on the same hardware. At that time, institutions typically had a single mainframe that could only be used by one person at a time. Time-sharing and virtualization techniques aimed to bypass this limit, splitting up resources and allocating them to users (see Fano and Corbató 1966). From very early on then, as Hu shows in his *Prehistory of the Cloud* (2015), computing was fixated on reducing "wasted" time and "idle" computing cycles. Virtualization partially addressed this problem by allowing "fixed units of labor and hardware to become mobile again" (Hu 2015, 62). Yet for several decades, hypervisors remained a niche implementation, only employed for high-end mainframes. It wasn't until hypervisors became available on commodity servers in the early 2000s that they became widely adopted in data centers. In late 2000, VMWare introduced its first server virtualization platform, followed by subsequent versions over the next years that introduced new features; in 2003, competitor Xen released its own virtualization offering, followed two months later by Microsoft (Marshall et al. 2008, 4–7). Already by 2005, virtualization was being recognized as a "killer app" (Loftus 2005).

In essence, hypervisors provided flexibility, decoupling hardware and software. A machine was no longer fixed as a Windows box with 8 GB of memory, for example. Instead, hypervisors could create multiple "virtual machines" on a single machine, each with its own operating system and allocation of resources. This ability allowed operators to combine multiple workloads onto fewer machines, improving efficiencies within the data center. For industry associations concerned with sustainability (Talaber et al. 2009): "Consolidation using virtualization is one powerful tool that can be applied to many data centers to drive up server efficiency and drive down energy consumption."

Yet these measures were still not enough. In their 2009 book on "warehouse-scale computing" Google engineers Hoelzle and Barroso quantified data center inefficiency. The engineers analyzed two clusters, each with 20,000 servers, over a two month period. The cluster with mixed workloads, including online services, was far from optimal in terms of efficiency. As the authors admit: "most of the time is spent within the 10–50% CPU utilization range," with an average of only around 30% use (Hoelzle and Barroso 2009, 108). If Google was the most open in admitting to inefficiency, it is not the only case. One study on public clouds found that the average utilization of ten Amazon Web Services servers was only around 7% (Liu 2011). And recent studies based on the Alibaba cluster data put its utilization at less than 17% (Lu et al. 2017). This low level of activity is only compounded by the design of servers, which are engineered for a high use case. As the Google engineers explain (Hoelzle and Barroso 2009, 108): "This activity profile turns out to be a perfect mismatch with the energy efficiency profile of modern servers in that they spend most of their time in the load region where they are most inefficient."

As data centers grew in both size and number over the next few years, their energy use came under increasing scrutiny. Rather than being merely an industry or academic concern, critiques began appearing in more mainstream avenues. A *US News and World Report* story in 2009 described data centers as "energy hogs," pointing to their rapidly growing demands and raising concerns about rolling blackouts and greenhouse gases (Garber 2009). In 2012, the *New York Times* conducted a yearlong investigation into data center energy use. As part of the story they asked McKinsey & Company to analyze data center energy use. The firm found that "on average, they were using only 6 percent to 12 percent of the electricity powering their servers to perform computations"; indeed, after compiling documents and conducting interviews, the journalists concluded that rather than the "image of sleek efficiency and environmental friendliness" that was usually portrayed, "most data centers, by design, consume vast amounts of energy in an incongruously wasteful manner" (Glanz 2012). A *Time* report the following year (Walsh 2013) echoed these findings, warning that "computers and smartphones might seem clean, but the digital economy uses a tenth of the world's electricity—and that share will only increase, with serious consequences for the economy and the environment."

"The data center needs an operating system," claimed Benjamin Hindman (2014) in a rather prescient and widely referenced article for O'Reilly Media: "It's time for applications—not servers—to rule the data center."[1] Hindman argued that the established understanding of the data center as a set of machines was fundamentally wrong. This mindset was encouraging developers to do the most logical thing when deploying their services—assign one application per machine. But as Hindman asked:

> What happens when a machine dies in one of these static partitions? Let's hope we over-provisioned sufficiently (wasting money), or can re-provision another machine quickly (wasting

effort). What about when the web traffic dips to its daily low? With static partitions we allocate for peak capacity, which means when traffic is at its lowest, all of that excess capacity is wasted. This is why a typical data center runs at only 8–15% efficiency.

For Hindman, hardware still dictated data center operations, imposing a machine-by-machine architecture that prevented it from performing to its true potential. This inflexibility was producing inefficiency. Instead, storage and processing capacity should be understood and managed as fluid resources. Compute should be malleable, able to be rapidly redeployed as needed. In essence, Hindman's vision consisted of two steps: "Pool together the basic compute resources from multiple data center clusters into a single virtual infrastructure. Then distribute scalable workloads throughout that pool and continually manage them for efficiency" (Fulton 2017).

Bringing this rhetoric down to earth somewhat, Hindman's "data center operating system" was a container cluster manager. Rather than isolated machines running individual software, the cluster manager functions as a kind of conductor, orchestrating their scheduling and execution of all the workloads and services running on a cluster (Fulton 2019). On a technical level, rather than hypervisor-based virtualization, it was container-based virtualization (see van Kessel 2016). Hindman's own product, Mesos DC/OS, joins a marketplace of other container cluster managers like Docker Swarm and Kubernetes. The latter, while now widely adopted by companies and a developer community, is an open-source version of Google's own cluster management tool that it had used in-house for years (Verma et al. 2015; Burns et al. 2016).

Alibaba also runs its own cluster management system, which consists of agents and schedulers. In 2015, in an effort to increase efficiency, the company came up with a plan to combine two types of jobs into the same cluster. Broadly speaking, jobs in the data center can be divided into two types. First, there are online service jobs. These are consumer facing and so often require low latency in order to function and feel responsive. For instance, this might be an e-commerce service that processes the credit cards of shoppers. These services are not typically processor intensive, but must remain continually on and constantly available, maintained around the clock. Their use will vary greatly, from a trickle of users to massive spikes in demand, requiring the ability to swiftly expand and grab more resources like storage and processors.

Indeed, the millions of online transactions during the "Double 11 Global Shopping Festival"—a major e-commerce event that now dwarfs Black Friday and Cyber Monday—provide one of the acid tests for these kinds of online service jobs.

Second, there are offline batch jobs. These are typically about processing information rather than providing a service. For this reason they are not consumer facing, nor time sensitive in the same way. Indeed, sometimes these are run as "nightlies," leveraging down time overnight in order to be available the next morning. These often take the form of highly processor intensive tasks: data mining of massive datasets, machine learning applications, large scale computing, and so on. To accelerate the completion of these jobs, the cloud can leverage parallel computing frameworks, where tasks are split into smaller subtasks, farmed out to many machines simultaneously, and then assembled back together again.

Typically these two types of jobs have been placed on separate clusters, or groups of machines. Yet if this separation was clean and straightforward conceptually, it was highly inefficient in terms of utilizing data center resources. A cluster dedicated only to offline batch jobs, for instance, would require cooling and power throughout the entire day, but might only be carrying out "real work" for a small portion of that time. Conversely, online services might not be using all the resources provisioned to them; this spare capacity could potentially be sunk into processor-intensive offline batch jobs. Both financially and environmentally, then, this architecture contributed toward significant wastefulness and a misuse of resources.

Co-allocation strives to remedy this problem. The basic concept is that both job types are allocated to the same cluster, allowing resources to be used where and when they are needed. Rather than sitting idle and draining power, machines should remain active, moving back and forth between offline and online jobs as needed. Co-allocation deploys "latency-insensitive offline batch computing tasks and latency-sensitive online services in the same batch of machines in Alibaba data centers," explains a page on Alibaba Developer (2019); in doing so, "idle resources not being used by online services can be used offline to improve the overall machine utilization rate." The next section steps through each data visualization in order to examine the successes and failures of this vision.

Visualizing (In)efficiency

The first image (Figure 3.1) shows 1,200 servers over the course of 11 hours, with each server represented by a single line. Every five minutes, the load of each server is polled. Load, in essence, is a figure expressing how many processes are waiting in the queue to access that server's processor. When the line spikes upwards, it indicates the server is under high load; when it dips down, the server's load is low at that point in time.

Looking across the image, what stands out is the many lines that almost perfectly mirror each other. Many lines follow the curves and undulations of the slopes above or below them. This pattern can be seen in the middle third of the image in particular. These matched lines show machines under a similar load pattern over the course of a day. This suggests that this group of machines has been assigned the same task—they are carrying out the same job for the same company. Rather than 1,200 individual machines, we see here the extent to which processing in the data center is coordinated.

This insight resonates with broader changes in the data center industry. While some data centers do host dozens of smaller companies, it is the hyperscalers—companies like Facebook, Google, and Amazon—that are understood to be driving growth. Tech giants may rent out entire floors of a data center, occupying much of its capacity with their outsized square footage and energy demands. "Only five years ago you felt a 250,000 sq ft building with 10MW was a lot" recalled one industry insider (Judge 2019), "now we may do a lease for 36MW for one client, and they'll take it in six rooms." Indeed, data centers actively pursue these kinds of "anchor tenants" for the guaranteed business and stability they provide.

The second image (Figure 3.2) draws upon the same dataset of 1,200 machines over 11 hours, but focuses on memory utilization. Each server contains a certain amount of total memory. As a job is executed, this memory fills up with the data and instructions related to the job. Memory usage is one indicator of the intensity of processing required to carry out a job. Processing a few fields like name and credit card for an online payment, for instance, would only take a tiny portion of memory. In contrast, sorting millions of rows of a database or transforming hours of video would be a highly memory-intensive job. Visually, this image takes the form of a heat-map. Hotter colors like yellow and orange indicate memory usage closer to 100%, while cooler shades of purple represent

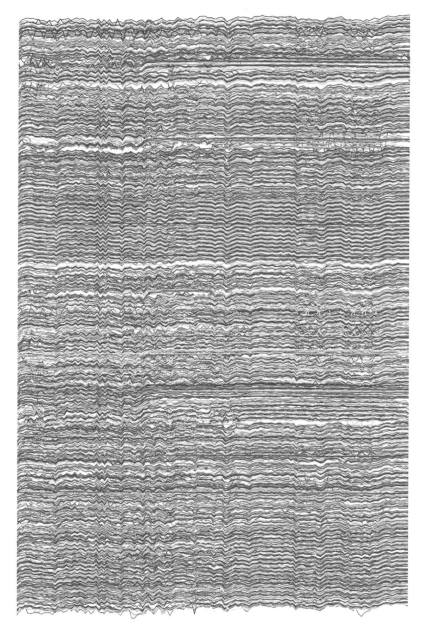

Figure 3.1 Server usage over 12 hours, with each line representing a server.

low memory use (white rectangles in this image indicate gaps in the data for small moments of time). Looking down the image, an uneven pattern immediately becomes apparent. On the one hand, we see a significant number of machines with hot colors throughout the 12 hours period. Oscillating between orange and yellow, these machines are almost constantly occupied with jobs that push their memory limits. Yet on the other hand, there are huge blocks of machines that remain purple or even black throughout the entire day. These machines are switched on—drawing power and costing the data center money—but are not carrying out any work for clients. According to the logic of efficiency, they are wasting resources.

This uneven performance in the Alibaba cluster has been pointed out by other researchers. In their paper, Lu and his co-authors (2017) described an "imbalance in the cloud." This consists first in Spatial Imbalance. Ideally, the work scheduler would use all of the machines—the full "space" of computing resources—equally. Yet, echoing the finding above, the authors noted the "heterogeneous resource utilization across machines and workloads" (2802). In other words, some machines are constantly churning, while others lie almost dormant for the entire day. Second, the authors noted a Temporal Imbalance, with "greatly time-varying resource usages per workload and machine" (2802). As will be shown in the next image, some jobs require minutes or even hours, while others take less than a second. Finally, the authors observed the "Imbalanced proportion of multi-dimensional resources (CPU and memory) utilization per workload" (2802). Jobs tend to drastically over-reserve resources like the processor and memory, only to use a tiny proportion of their allocated amount when they are actually run. More accurate estimates would leave more computation resources available, allowing other jobs to take up these resources and be completed.

The third image (Figure 3.3) shows the particular CPUs assigned to jobs over the 12 hour period. CPU is short for central processing unit, and can be understood colloquially as the brains of the machine, the core component that carries out calculations. In this cluster, a job can be assigned to any one of 64 total machines, represented by 64 lines from left to right. In practice, jobs are typically assigned to four or eight CPUs at a time, indicated by four or eight lines next to each other. By scrolling down the image, we can see the ways in which jobs are allocated throughout the day.

While the resulting image is rather complex, the key point here is that Alibaba's allocation system is attempting to balance CPU

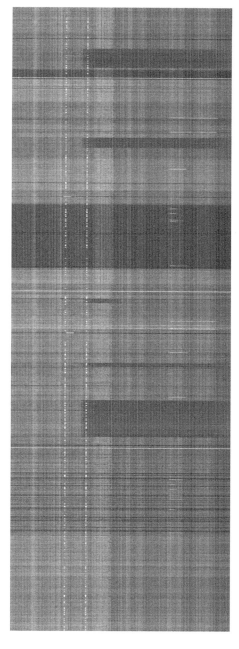

Figure 3.2 Heat-map visualization of memory usage over time, with one row per machine.

Figure 3.3 (detail). Visualization showing which of the 64 CPUs are assigned to each job.

use across the cluster. A perfectly load balanced cluster strives to equally allocate jobs, giving new jobs to unused CPUs—in this visualization, to never have repeating lines. However, scrolling down the image reveals a number of thick black repeating lines, showing where the same group of CPUs has been selected over and over to carry out each new job. As this group is repeatedly hit with new work, we could assume that its temperature rises and more cooling is needed, requiring in turn more energy. This trend becomes acute at the very end of the day (the bottom of the image), where long black squares show how CPUs #44–#64 are repeatedly pummeled by new jobs, while the rest of the CPUs in the cluster go entirely unused.

The fourth image (Figure 3.4) focuses on the timing and duration of tasks that machines carry out. Over the same 12 hour period, this production cluster carried out around 13,000 tasks. The data provided by Alibaba logs when the task began and when it was completed. Visually, each task is depicted by a colored line, with the entire image representing a timeline of the day moving from left to right.

Here, as mentioned above, we can witness the temporal imbalance pointed out by Lu and colleagues. The red line near the top, for instance, displays a task that takes several hours to complete, while the blips and dots that punctuate the image indicate jobs that last only seconds. Of particular note is the task "waterfall," the cascade of lines that occurs toward the end of the day. Looking down the image, an almost identical cascade can be seen in the same period over and over again. As discussed in the first image, this sequence of short tasks is a highly coordinated level of processing, suggesting a single client with nearly identical jobs to be completed.

The fifth image (Figure 3.5) focuses on the status of 1 million Alibaba instances over time. Each pixel is one instance. Ready and Waiting instances are displayed in gray, Running in green, Terminated and Failed in red, and Cancelled and Interrupted in orange. While green dominates the image, indicating that most instances complete with no issues, a number of red and gray dots also show that waiting and failed instances are not uncommon.

The sixth and final image (Figure 3.6) is a relatively technical interrogation. MPKI is short for missed-predictions-per-thousand (k)-instructions. This industry metric refers to the ability of a processor to carry out branch prediction. To achieve optimal processing, this number should be as close to zero as possible, with no missed predictions. Visually, the color scheme here ranges from blue to pink, using a scale of 0–20 MPKI. Certainly the sea of blue

Figure 3.4 (detail). Gantt-style display of the timing and duration of tasks over a 12 hour period.

Figure 3.5 The status of 1 million instances, with color indicating completion, waiting, or error.

in the image indicates very low misses and high processor performance. Yet the dappled pink dots interspersed throughout show that processing is not perfect, and up to 20 predictions per 1,000 can be missed at times.

Alibaba's vision was to increase efficiency through co-allocation. Efficiency here, as elsewhere, would entail a smooth, ceaseless productivity, where disruption of any kind would be avoided. In her book-length study on the history of efficiency, Jennifer Alexander

Figure 3.6 Displays the "perfection" of processing gauged by the level of missed-predictions-per-thousand instructions.

(2008, 163) defines the ideal of efficiency as "a process fully understood and fully predictable, disrupted neither by unknown movements nor by particular or unique ones." Depending on the industry, such disruptions may take the form of a mechanical failure, an unruly child, or an unforeseen natural disaster. These disruptions emerge from unwanted developments or unexpected catastrophes, from "externalities" that interrupt the seamless operations that are desired.

Perhaps one of the most striking dynamics observed in these images, then, is the way that work itself disrupts efficiency. Work on a data center cluster, as discussed earlier, takes the form of jobs and tasks. Certainly these can all be completed on the "universal machine" of the computer servers. Yet far from being homogenous, the visualizations above together demonstrate the highly heterogeneous nature of these jobs. Some require hours to calculate, others a few seconds. Some are computationally intensive, while others use a fraction of their allocated memory. Some must respond "in the moment" to customers; others are offline batches, free to run overnight. Alibaba attempts to allocate these jobs to the cluster, but these highly diverse forms of work essentially stretch the scheduler, they introduce resource conflicts, and they overwhelm its ability to efficiently orchestrate work.

Several papers examining the Alibaba dataset have recognized the disruption this work causes, even if they are framed in the more technical language of computer science. One of the first analyses argued that the co-allocation approach creates a number of fundamental imbalances across the cluster. "Such imbalances exacerbate the complexity and challenge of cloud resource management, which might incur severe wastes of resources and low cluster utilization" (Lu et al. 2017). After analyzing the cluster data, Ren and co-authors (2018) similarly concluded that: "Unavoidably, deploying multiple applications to share resources on the same node will cause contentions and performance tilt." The mixture of two job types, as Jiang et al. (2019) observe, results "in scheduling complexity and interferences among online services and batch jobs." The divergence of these tasks introduces a degree of contingency into the system that cannot be anticipated nor managed. In doing so, these jobs frustrate the control necessary for optimal productivity. Work itself proves disruptive to efficiency.

Inhuman Efficiency

In data center rhetoric, there is a clear figure responsible for these inefficiencies—the human. The data center has become a highly complex environment, with countless tasks, each with their own demands, running across hundreds or even thousands of machines. Yet the prioritization and execution of jobs are still determined manually, for example via rulesets set out by the operator or on a case-by-case, cluster-by-cluster basis. Pundits have begun to deride this practice as antiquated or even artisanal. These are "hand-edited algorithm schedules" (Nelson 2019) or a "hand-rolled container stack" (Wells 2019). For critics, this traditional approach requires significant amounts of tedious work. This work cannot be carried out by anyone, but requires the expertise of a highly trained (and highly paid) individual. Clients need to be considered, job patterns understood, and underlying resources properly leveraged. As Mao et al (2019) acknowledge, "workload-specific scheduling policies that use this information require expert knowledge and significant effort to devise, implement, and validate."

While human labor is expensive and time-consuming, the larger problem for these commentators is that it is fundamentally ineffective. Human engineers cannot adequately grasp the complexities of the data center and the myriad variables around jobs, resources, and priorities. As one commentator observed: "Unfathomable permutations for humans in the manually edited scheduling can include the fact that a lower node (smaller computational task) can't start work until an upper node (larger, more power-requiring computational task) has completed its work" (Nelson 2019). When humans undertake this work, they produce task schedules that are straightforward to understand but ultimately inefficient. Often based on observation and trial and error, they are "clever heuristics for a simplified model of the problem" (Mao et al. 2016, 50). In following this schedule, computable resources lie underutilized even as they continue to drain power and require cooling.

A new array of automated solutions have begun to encroach on this space. In 2014, "Tetris" drew from a parallel problem of bin packing, "packing" jobs as tightly as possible and adaptively learning task requirements as it went (Grandl et al. 2014). In 2016, "DeepRM" drew more specifically from machine learning techniques; after training it began holding back large jobs to make room for soon-to-arrive smaller jobs, a sophisticated strategy that was learned automatically (Mao et al. 2016, 55). These precedents culminated in "Decima," a neural net-based approach that automatically learns how to optimally allocate workloads across thousands of servers (Mao et al. 2019; see also Matheson 2019). Echoing the human-as-problem rhetoric above, commentators noted how "Decima can find opportunities for [scheduling] optimization that are simply too onerous to realize via manual design/tuning processes" (Nelson 2019).

For industry proponents, then, efficiency is an important problem best tackled by machines. Indeed, the shift to containerization suggests that these issues are not so much beyond humans as beneath them. While these problems are complex, they are also mundane and low level, not worth attending to. In an interview, Hindman compares the advent of these virtual containers to the advent of virtual memory. Memory was once a scarce resource that was also allocated "by hand," with programmers manually tracking where variables and datasets were stored. If this granted total control, it was also highly time-consuming and required meticulous attention to detail. Virtual memory not only abstracted away hardware memory but also allowed it to be pooled and managed automatically. In the same vein, data center operating systems and container managers abstract away servers and their low-level specifics. "Containers encapsulate the application environment" asserts Burns et al (2016), "abstracting away many details of machines and operating systems from the application developer and the deployment infrastructure." In this vision, developers and engineers should not have to worry about trivial details like individual machines and their hardware resources. Instead, compute should be flexible, automatically adapting to the requirements of any given task and efficiently carrying it out. As Hindman's interviewer (Hindman 2015) concluded: "People are going to have to get over their own 'perceived' expertise and let computers do stuff that they're good at."

According to this imaginary, what humans are good at is strategizing, innovating, and creating. Not only are these tasks difficult to automate, but they are the kind of high-level cognitive labor that disrupts incumbents, invents services, and opens markets, generating more sustainable and profitable value. These technologies carry out a double move: designating efficiency as a low-level machinic problem "frees up" the human to concentrate on more "meaningful" and "productive" work. "It is for reasons of productivity that the cloud is designed to remove infrastructure from sight," notes Hu (2015, 62), "so that its users can focus on higher-level applications—namely, more 'useful' jobs that lift users from the factory floor and toward the noble air of the knowledge economy." In this sense, the technology sector dovetails neatly into a broader program of neoliberal capitalism (Boltanski and Chiapello 2017), where individuals are liberated from mundane labor in order to create more inspired and entrepreneurial forms of value.

Questioning Efficiency

Taken together, the data visualizations above demonstrate that—despite the best efforts of data center engineers over several years to schedule jobs and allocate resources in an optimal way—inefficiencies remain significant. Yet more fundamentally, we might ask why efficiency is the frame we are offered to understand these technical (but always also social and political) systems. What work does this frame do, what does it show and hide, and how might we question it?

On an immediate level, efficiency provides a powerful paradigm, establishing a problem, a goal, and a clear path forward. As Wajcman notes (2015, 178), efficiency slots into a broader framework "in which technical rationality both defines political problems and provides the solution." Efficiency points out the "waste" of energy, the glut of time, the misuse of resources. If these are the issues, then the solution becomes equally concrete: become more efficient. Computer scientists and software engineers are good at efficiency. Current performance can be quantitatively tested, providing a baseline. Every possible optimization—newer hardware, innovations in software, advanced schedulers—can then be measured against this benchmark. Improvements are retained; unsuccessful experiments are discarded. The result is an incremental but steady advancement, a sense of verifiable progression. These gains can then be touted in trade journals or in the press releases of hyperscalers like Google, Amazon Web Services, or Alibaba itself.

One of the key strengths of efficiency is its flexibility. While Alibaba's data center clusters are the focus here, the efficiency imperative might equally be applied to a supply chain, a civic initiative, or a public transport network. Efficiency is reflexive, hermetic even, positing an enclosed system and measuring itself by its own inputs and outputs. The general concept of efficiency, explains Jennifer Alexander (2008, 165), enabled "the assessment of almost any action or process on the basis of the same units and qualities it had started with and nothing else." Efficiency always points back to itself, aiming to accomplish the same task faster, or with the use of less resources, or at vaster scales. In this sense, efficiency is content agnostic. It can serve as an envelope for any process, from any industry. Efficiency is an off-the-shelf vision, already embedded with values, milestones, and regimes of measurement, that can be applied to anything. However, if efficiency offers an enticing frame, it is also a particular one. In imposing a new, overarching set of values, efficiency suppresses alternative ways of understanding it. Alibaba never speaks about the specifics of their data center operations—the data being harvested, the capital being funneled, the personal information being onsold—but only observes that these processes could be more efficiently managed. In this sense, efficiency acts as a wrapper, shrouding original values and norms. As Feenberg (1996, 53) notes, moral and ethical outcomes are "occluded rather than revealed by the application of technical norms." Efficiency is an apolitical envelope that obscures the politics of systems and processes. Feenberg (1996, 54) stresses that "considerations of efficiency are invoked to remove issues from normative judgment and public discussion." Former qualms are rendered irrelevant; a new set of metrics for measuring success is introduced. Efficiency is strategic in foregrounding technical rationality while sidelining messier questions around labor and capital, inequality and sociality, privacy and the public good.

Indeed, one of the red threads running through social science critiques of efficiency is this idea that efficiency both highlights and obscures. Efficiency is a powerful conceptual frame, admits Lutzenhiser (2014, 143), but precisely because it "seems to illuminate the world so clearly... other aspects seem to disappear." Efficiency makes sense of the world, yet simultaneously marginalizes other perspectives. Efficiency literature is dominated by narrowly focused "techno-economic approaches" that fail to account for its complex contexts and societal tradeoffs (Dunlop 2019). Because of this, many sociological critiques reiterate the same point: (energy) "efficiency tends to obfuscate wider societal issues—specifically those concerning energy justice, environmental and philosophical concerns" (Dunlop 2019, 8). As STS scholar Langdon Winner (1980, 256) once asserted, to focus solely on efficiency is to miss "a decisive element in the story."

What does efficiency obscure? On an immediate level, it obscures the target of efficiency. What is being made more efficient, for whom, and to what end? In the data center industry as well as the broader technology sector, these questions are often never asked. It is axiomatic that PUE (power usage effectiveness) ratios should continue to drop, that new techniques for maximizing power and cooling should be welcomed, and that "better" schedulers and software should be embraced. Viewed through the framing of efficiency, the data center industry appears to be improving every year. Progress is being made. Yet again this view is highly insular, neglecting to consider the aims and intentions of these processes. What is being done is irrelevant; all that matters is that it is done faster and with less resources. It is efficiency stripped of any context—efficiency for efficiency's sake.

Against this bracketed view, we can consider what these data infrastructures accomplish and what the sociopolitical impacts of these operations are. Without a doubt, the largest and fastest growing data center segment are the "hyperscale" (Miller 2019) companies mentioned earlier, tech giants such as Google, Amazon, Facebook, Apple, and Alibaba who either construct their own massive facilities or rent and manage floors of space from existing providers. These platforms and services are based upon an invasive and exploitative business model, where user data is harvested, assembled, packaged, and then sold onto third-party advertisers (Pasquinelli 2009; Fuchs 2014; Morozov 2014; Srnicek 2017). As Scholz (2016) argues, these entities "insert themselves between those who offer services and others who are looking for them, thereby embedding extractive processes into social interaction." Alongside their consumer-facing services, companies like Google and Facebook have invested heavily in machine learning architectures, where data is mined in order to produce more invasive insights into consumers (Metz 2016). These dynamics produce a highly asymmetric internet, where users offer up their personal data for access into the "walled gardens" offered by a handful of tech corporations. Underpinned by data center processes, these environments are "predicated upon an unprecedented intensification of extractive dynamics and related processes of dispossession" (Neilson and Mezzadra 2017). With this in mind, making the data center more efficient equates to making these exploitative processes faster and less resource-intensive. It means "packing" this work in more sophisticated ways, allowing more work to be accomplished. In effect, it means an optimization of extraction.

Efficiency, then, is not an end to itself, but must be understood in relation to what is being made efficient. As Winner (1980, 121) stressed, these technologies should be judged "not only for their contributions to efficiency and productivity and their positive and negative environmental side effects, but also for the ways in which they can embody specific forms of power and authority." The capture of data, the extraction of social processes, and the funneling of capital carried out by hyperscale companies are problematic, if not pathological. In this sense, efficiency is neither apolitical nor objective, but rather deeply intertwined with the values, norms, and visions of those it services.

More broadly, efficiency aligns with capitalism and its imperative of productivity. There is a long lineage of criticism wary of efficiency and the exploitative potential of machinic regimes. Marx recognized the double-edged nature of efficiency—more efficient machines pressured the laborer to keep up, to maintain the pace and intensity of work. While output would be increased, the exploitation of the laborer and the toll on her body would also increase (Marx 2004, 829–830). For Ellul (1967, 188), individuals were subordinated to technical progress and its all-consuming "calculus of efficiency." Similarly for Ivan Illich (1973, 10), machines removed the creativity and autonomy necessary for fulfilling labor, enslaving men. For Wajcman (2015, 162), efficiency is a "dominant engineering approach" that attempts to save and order the time of social life. (For a survey of similar critiques, see Zoellich and Bisht 2018.) These critiques caution against efficiency, its economic logics, and its obsession with productivity. They worry that human life will become diminished. Filtered through this starkly quantitative lens, the richness of human sociality, language, and labor will be reduced to a set of inputs and outputs. Popular literature has picked up these critiques in simplistic ways. To resist these stressful, destructive regimes, we need to waste time (Lightman 2018), learn to do nothing (Odell 2018), and step back and slow down (Jonat 2018). Inefficiency should be embraced.

Yet if these concerns are understandable, they are also entrenched in a history of human-centered labor. How might Alibaba's facility challenge these understandings? Can wasted machinic time really still be theorized through Taylorism? Can an "idle" machine still be understood through a Weberian critique of work-ethic? The Alibaba compute cluster is a pool of machines where jobs are assigned and completed, manipulating, transforming, and processing data, until each task is complete. While engineers may function at the edges of this regime, checking services and maintaining hardware, this labor is decidedly machine-centered rather than human-centered.

Indeed, one of the clear pushes of the data center industry is to more comprehensively automate these facilities. Systems should carry out predictive maintenance and algorithms should automatically control cooling, forming an auto-healing, auto-optimized environment (Miller 2019). These initiatives move toward the compelling vision of the "lights out" data center (Donoghue 2017; Carlini 2020). In this dream, on-site staff, even now typically just a handful of workers, will no longer be necessary. Server maintenance can be automated or completed remotely. The vestigial human and the concession to her vision can finally be jettisoned. Operations run smoothly and incessantly in the dark.

Of course, this is not to claim that a machine-centric shift resolves the issue of efficiency. Critique is still necessary, and as the data center and its role proliferates, attending to the processes at the heart of these environments, as noted above, will become even more urgent. It is simply to note that the question of efficiency in this machinic realm feels like a different kind of question. Here, theorizations based on 19th- and 20th-century human-centric labor regimes begin to fray at the edges. Arguments based heavily on efficiency impinging human creativity and autonomy start to unravel. What is needed is a critical media theory grounded in a rich lineage of social theory, yet also aware of the promising possibilities ushered in by these technical architectures and operations.

Visualizing Alibaba's cluster dataset provides insight into the operations and contradictions at the heart of the data center. Data center efficiency, centering around machine utilization rates, has long been an acknowledged problem in the industry. Alibaba's vision of co-allocation aimed to address this issue by combining online and offline jobs. However, as the data visualizations demonstrated, this move introduces new forms of complexity. Jobs are highly heterogeneous in their durations and demands, creating difficulties in scheduling and conflicts in allocation. Work itself proves to be a disruption to efficiency. For the industry, this complexity confirms that efficiency is an issue for machines, driving automated schedulers and new layers of abstraction that allow operators to devote themselves to more productive and "high impact" labor. After exploring these dynamics, the chapter questioned the framing of efficiency itself. While efficiency can be justified on an economic and environmental level, its merit is often assumed. Efficiency introduces a particular framing, defining a problem, establishing a goal, and offering a compelling road map to achieving it. Yet if efficiency is clarifying, it is also obfuscating, bracketing out alternative ways of understanding these sociotechnical systems. As hyperscale companies dominate data centers, what is being made efficient are operations that are often exploitative and invasive. Efficiency, then, should certainly be critiqued and questioned. Yet to merely valorize inefficiency is to all-too-quickly fall back on comfortable tropes. As the data center grows in significance while de-centering human labor, it becomes important to develop a critical theorization of efficiency attuned to the new conditions of this machine-centric future.

Note

1 The same phrase—"The Datacenter Needs an Operating System"—actually appears in an earlier 2011 conference paper by Zaharia and Hindman, along with several co-authors.

References

Alexander, Jennifer Karns. 2008. *The Mantra of Efficiency: From Waterwheel to Social Control.* Baltimore, MD: Johns Hopkins University Press.

Alibaba. (2017) 2019. *Alibaba/Clusterdata.* Alibaba. https://github.com/alibaba/clusterdata.

Alibaba Developer. 2019. "Alibaba Cluster Data: Using 270 GB of Open Source Data to Understand Alibaba Data Centers." Alibaba Cloud Community. January 7, 2019. https://www.alibabacloud.com/blog/alibaba-cluster-data-using-270-gb-of-open-source-data-to-understand-alibaba-data-centers_594340.

Andrae, Anders S. G., and Tomas Edler. 2015. "On Global Electricity Usage of Communication Technology: Trends to 2030." *Challenges* 6 (1): 117–57. https://doi.org/10.3390/challe6010117.

Boltanski, Luc, and Eve Chiapello. 2017. *The New Spirit of Capitalism.* Translated by Gregory Elliot. London: Verso.

Burns, Brendan, Brian Grant, David Oppenheimer, Eric Brewer, and John Wilkes. 2016. "Borg, Omega, and Kubernetes." *Queue* 14 (1): 70–93.

Carlini, Steven. 2020. "Why Every Data Center in the Future Will Be 'Lights Out.'" Schneider Electric Blog. June 22, 2020. https://blog.se.com/datacenter/2020/06/22/why-every-data-center-in-the-future-will-be-lights-out/.

Cheng, Yue, Ali Anwar, and Xuejing Duan. 2018. "Analyzing Alibaba's Co-Located Datacenter Workloads." In *2018 IEEE International Conference on Big Data (Big Data)*, 292–97. Seattle, WA: IEEE. https://doi.org/10.1109/BigData.2018.8622518.

Daggett, Cara New. 2019. *The Birth of Energy: Fossil Fuels, Thermodynamics, and the Politics of Work.* Durham, NC: Duke University Press.

Davis, Charles R. 1985. "A Critique of the Ideology of Efficiency." *Humboldt Journal of Social Relations* 12 (2): 73–86.

Delforge, Pierre. 2015. "America's Data Centers Consuming and Wasting Growing Amounts of Energy." NRDC. February 6, 2015. https://www.nrdc.org/resources/americas-data-centers-consuming-and-wasting-growing-amounts-energy.

Donoghue, Andrew. 2017. "Beyond Lights-Out: Future Data Centers Will Be Human-Free." Data Center Knowledge. September 19, 2017. https://www.datacenterknowledge.com/design/beyond-lights-out-future-data-centers-will-be-human-free.

Dunlop, Tessa. 2019. "Mind the Gap: A Social Sciences Review of Energy Efficiency." *Energy Research & Social Science* 56 (October): 1–12. https://doi.org/10.1016/j.erss.2019.05.026.

Ellul, Jacques. 1964. *The Technological Society*. New York: Vintage.

Fano, R. M., and F. J. Corbató. 1966. "Time-Sharing on Computers." *Scientific American* 215 (3): 128–43.

Feenberg, Andrew. 1996. "Marcuse or Habermas: Two Critiques of Technology." *Inquiry* 39 (1): 45–70. https://doi.org/10.1080/00201749608602407.

Flucker, Sophia, Robert Tozer, and Beth Whitehead. 2018. "Data Centre Sustainability – Beyond Energy Efficiency." *Building Services Engineering Research and Technology* 39 (2): 173–82. https://doi.org/10.1177/0143624417753022.

Fuchs, Christian. 2014. *Digital Labour and Karl Marx*. London: Routledge.

Fulton, Scott. 2017. "One Year In, Has DC/OS Changed the Data Center?" Data Center Knowledge. April 24, 2017. https://www.datacenterknowledge.com/archives/2017/04/24/one-year-dcos-changed-data-center.

———. 2019. "What Is Kubernetes? How Orchestration Redefines the Data Center." ZDNet. April 25, 2019. https://www.zdnet.com/article/what-kubernetes-really-is-and-how-orchestration-redefines-the-data-center/.

Garber, Kent. 2009. "The Internet's Hidden Energy Hogs: Data Servers." *US News & World Report*, March 24, 2009. https://www.usnews.com/news/energy/articles/2009/03/24/the-internets-hidden-energy-hogs-data-servers.

Glanz, James. 2012. "Data Centers Waste Vast Amounts of Energy, Belying Industry Image." *The New York Times*, September 22, 2012. http://www.nytimes.com/2012/09/23/technology/data-centers-waste-vast-amounts-of-energy-belying-industry-image.html.

Grandl, Robert, Ganesh Ananthanarayanan, Srikanth Kandula, Sriram Rao, and Aditya Akella. 2014. "Multi-Resource Packing for Cluster Schedulers." In *Proceedings of the 2014 ACM Conference on SIGCOMM - SIGCOMM '14*, 455–66. Chicago, Illinois, USA: ACM Press. https://doi.org/10.1145/2619239.2626334.

Hatzenbuehler, Anthony. 2018. "The Importance of Uptime and All Those Nines." CoreSite. March 5, 2018. https://www.coresite.com/blog/the-importance-of-uptime-and-all-those-nines.

Hindman, Benjamin. 2014. "Why the Data Center Needs an Operating System." O'Reilly Media. December 3, 2014. https://www.oreilly.com/ideas/why-the-data-center-needs-an-operating-system.

Hindman, with Benjamin. 2015. a16z Podcast: The Datacenter Needs an Operating System Interview by Steven Sinofsky. https://a16z.com/2015/01/05/a16z-podcast-why-the-datacenter-needs-an-operating-system/.

Hoelzle, Urs, and Luiz Andre Barroso. 2009. *The Datacenter as a Computer: An Introduction to the Design of Warehouse-Scale Machines.* San Rafael, CA: Morgan and Claypool Publishers.

Holt, Jennifer, and Patrick Vonderau. 2015. "'Where the Internet Lives': Data Centers as Cloud Infrastructure." In *Signal Traffic: Critical Studies of Media Infrastructures*, edited by Lisa Parks and Nicole Starosielski, 175–229. Chicago: University of Illinois Press.

Hu, Tung-Hui. 2015. *A Prehistory of the Cloud.* Cambridge, MA: MIT Press.

Illich, Ivan. 1973. *Tools for Conviviality.* New York: Harper and Row.

Jaureguialzo, Enrique. 2011. "PUE: The Green Grid Metric for Evaluating the Energy Efficiency in DC (Data Center). Measurement Method Using the Power Demand." In *2011 IEEE 33rd International Telecommunications Energy Conference*, 1–8. https://doi.org/10.1109/INTLEC.2011.6099718.

Jiang, Congfeng, Guangjie Han, Jiangbin Lin, Gangyong Jia, Weisong Shi, and Jian Wan. 2019. "Characteristics of Co-Allocated Online Services and Batch Jobs in Internet Data Centers: A Case Study from Alibaba Cloud." *IEEE Access* 7: 22495–508. https://doi.org/10.1109/ACCESS.2019.2897898.

Jonat, Rachel. 2017. *The Joy of Doing Nothing: A Real-Life Guide to Stepping Back, Slowing Down, and Creating a Simpler, Joy-Filled Life.* New York: Adams Media.

Jörgenson, Loki, B. C. Ronald Kriz, Barbara Mones-Hattal, Bernice Rogowitz, and F. David Fracchia. 1995. "Panel: Is Visualization Struggling under the Myth of Objectivity?" In *Proceedings of the 6th Conference on Visualization '95*, 412. VIS '95. USA: IEEE Computer Society.

Judge, Peter. 2019. "How Webscale Is Swallowing Colo." Data Center Dynamics. May 17, 2019. https://www.datacenterdynamics.com/analysis/how-webscale-swallowing-colo/.

Kanev, Svilen, Juan Pablo Darago, Kim Hazelwood, Parthasarathy Ranganathan, Tipp Moseley, Gu-Yeon Wei, and David Brooks. 2015. "Profiling a Warehouse-Scale Computer." In *Proceedings of the 42nd Annual International Symposium on Computer Architecture - ISCA '15*, 158–69. Portland, Oregon: ACM Press. https://doi.org/10.1145/2749469.2750392.

Keim, Daniel, Huamin Qu, and Kwan-Liu Ma. 2013. "Big-Data Visualization." *IEEE Computer Graphics and Applications* 33 (4): 20–21.

Kosara, Robert. 2008. "The Unbearable Subjectivity of Visualization." *Eagereyes.* January 17, 2008. https://eagereyes.org/blog/2008/subjectivity-of-visualization.

54 *Efficiency and Waste*

Lightman, Alan. 2018. *In Praise of Wasting Time*. New York: Simon & Schuster/ TED.

Liu, Huan. 2011. "A Measurement Study of Server Utilization in Public Clouds." In, 435–42. IEEE.

Loftus, Jack. 2005. "Xen Virtualization Quickly Becoming Open Source 'Killer App.'" SearchDataCenter. December 19, 2005. https:// searchdatacenter.techtarget.com/news/1153127/Xen-virtualization-quickly-becoming-open-source-killer-app.

Lu, Chengzhi, Kejiang Ye, Guoyao Xu, Cheng-Zhong Xu, and Tongxin Bai. 2017. "Imbalance in the Cloud: An Analysis on Alibaba Cluster Trace." In *2017 IEEE International Conference on Big Data*, 2884–92. Boston, MA: IEEE. https://doi.org/10.1109/BigData.2017.8258257.

Lutzenhiser, Loren. 2014. "Through the Energy Efficiency Looking Glass." *Energy Research & Social Science* 1 (March): 141–51. https://doi. org/10.1016/j.erss.2014.03.011.

Mao, Hongzi, Mohammad Alizadeh, Ishai Menache, and Srikanth Kandula. 2016. "Resource Management with Deep Reinforcement Learning." In *Proceedings of the 15th ACM Workshop on Hot Topics in Networks - HotNets '16*, 50–56. Atlanta, GA: ACM Press. https://doi. org/10.1145/3005745.3005750.

Mao, Hongzi, Malte Schwarzkopf, Shaileshh Bojja Venkatakrishnan, Zili Meng, and Mohammad Alizadeh. 2019. "Learning Scheduling Algorithms for Data Processing Clusters." In *Proceedings of the ACM Special Interest Group on Data Communication - SIGCOMM '19*, 270–88. Beijing, China: ACM Press. https://doi.org/10.1145/3341302.3342080.

Marshall, David, Stephen S. Beaver, and Jason W. McCarty. 2008. *VMware ESX Essentials in the Virtual Data Center*. Boca Raton, FL: CRC Press.

Marwah, Manish, Bruno Silva, Sérgio Galdino, Jose Pires, Paulo Maciel, Amip Shah, Ratnesh Sharma, et al. 2010. "Quantifying the Sustainability Impact of Data Center Availability." *ACM SIGMETRICS Performance Evaluation Review* 37 (4): 64. https://doi.org/10.1145/1773394.1773405.

Marx, Karl. 2004. *Capital: A Critique of Political Economy*. Translated by Ben Fowkes. London: Penguin Books.

Matheson, Rob. 2019. "Artificial Intelligence Could Help Data Centers Run Far More Efficiently." MIT News. August 21, 2019. http://news.mit. edu/2019/decima-data-processing-0821.

Metz, Cade. 2016. "Google, Facebook, and Microsoft Are Remaking Themselves Around AI." *Wired*, November 21, 2016. https://www.wired. com/2016/11/google-facebook-microsoft-remaking-around-ai/.

Mezzadra, Sandro, and Brett Neilson. 2017. "On the Multiple Frontiers of Extraction: Excavating Contemporary Capitalism." *Cultural Studies* 31 (2–3): 185–204. https://doi.org/10.1080/09502386.2017.1303425.

Miller, Rich. 2019a. "What's Next for AI in Data Center Automation?" *Data Center Frontier* (blog). March 20, 2019. https://datacenterfrontier. com/whats-next-for-ai-in-data-center-automation/.

————. 2019b. "Hyperscale Data Centers." New Jersey: Data Center Frontier. https://datacenterfrontier.com/wp-content/uploads/2019/09/DCF-Special-Report-Hyperscale-Data-Centers.pdf.

Morozov, Evgeny. 2014. "Selling Your Bulk Online Data Really Means Selling Your Autonomy." *The New Republic*, May 14, 2014. https://newrepublic.com/article/117703/selling-personal-data-big-techs-war-meaning-life.

Nelson, Patrick. 2019. "Data Center-Specific AI Completes Tasks Twice as Fast." Network World. August 29, 2019. https://www.networkworld.com/article/3434597/data-center-specific-ai-completes-tasks-twice-as-fast.html.

Niccolai, James. 2013. "New Data Center Survey Shows Mediocre Results for Energy Efficiency." *Computerworld*. April 12, 2013. https://www.computerworld.com/article/2496597/new-data-center-survey-shows-mediocre-results-for-energy-efficiency.html.

Odell, Jenny. 2019. *How to Do Nothing: Resisting the Attention Economy.* Brooklyn, NY: Melville House.

Pasquinelli, Matteo. 2009. "Google's PageRank Algorithm: A Diagram of Cognitive Capitalism and the Rentier of the Common Intellect." In *Deep Search: The Politics of Search beyond Google*, edited by Konrad Becker and Felix Stalder, 152–62. London: Transaction Publishers.

Pinch, Trevor J. 1992. "Opening Black Boxes: Science, Technology and Society." *Social Studies of Science* 22 (3): 487–510. https://doi.org/10.1177/0306312792022003003.

Ren, Rui, Jinheng Li, Lei Wang, Jianfeng Zhan, and Zheng Cao. 2018. "Anomaly Analysis for Co-Located Datacenter Workloads in the Alibaba Cluster." *ArXiv:1811.06901 [Cs]*, November. http://arxiv.org/abs/1811.06901.

Riley, Judith Merkle. 1980. *Management and Ideology: The Legacy of the International Scientific Management Movement.* Berkeley: University of California Press.

Rossiter, Ned. 2017. *Software, Infrastructure, Labor: A Media Theory of Logistical Nightmares.* New York: Routledge.

Ruppert, Evelyn, Engin Isin, and Didier Bigo. 2017. "Data Politics." *Big Data & Society* 4 (2): 1–7.

Scholz, Trebor. 2016. "Platform Cooperativism." New York: Rosa Luxemburg Foundation. http://www.rosalux-nyc.org/wp-content/files_mf/scholz_platformcoop_5.9.2016.pdf.

Srnicek, Nick. 2017. *Platform Capitalism.* Cambridge: Polity Press.

Talaber, Richard, Tom Brey, and Larry Lamers. 2009. "Using Virtualization to Improve Data Center Efficiency." Washington, D.C.: The Green Grid.

Townend, Paul, Stephen Clement, Dan Burdett, Renyu Yang, Joe Shaw, Brad Slater, and Jie Xu. 2019. "Invited Paper: Improving Data Center Efficiency Through Holistic Scheduling In Kubernetes." In *2019 IEEE International Conference on Service-Oriented System Engineering (SOSE)*, 156–161. San Francisco East Bay, CA: IEEE. https://doi.org/10.1109/SOSE.2019.00030.

Uddin, Mueen, Jamshed Memon, Mohd Zaidi, Mohd Zaidi Abd Rozan, and Amjad Rehman. 2015. "Virtualised Load Management Algorithm to Reduce CO2 Emissions in the Data Centre Industry." *International Journal of Global Warming* 7 (January): 3–20. https://doi.org/10.1504/IJGW.2015.067413.

Uptime Institute. 2018. "Tier Classification System." May 21, 2018. https://uptimeinstitute.com/tiers.

Van Kessel, Jeroen. 2016. "Power Efficiency of Hypervisor-Based Virtualization versus Container-Based Virtualization." Amsterdam: University of Amsterdam. https://www.delaat.net/rp/2015-2016/p33/report.pdf.

Veel, Kristen. 2017. "Uncertain Architectures: Performing Shelter and Exposure." *Imaginations* 8 (2). http://imaginations.glendon.yorku.ca/?p=9956.

Verma, Abhishek, Luis Pedrosa, Madhukar Korupolu, David Oppenheimer, Eric Tune, and John Wilkes. 2015. "Large-Scale Cluster Management at Google with Borg." In *Proceedings of the Tenth European Conference on Computer Systems*, 1–17. EuroSys '15. Bordeaux, France: Association for Computing Machinery. https://doi.org/10.1145/2741948.2741964.

Wajcman, Judy. 2015. *Pressed for Time: The Acceleration of Life in Digital Capitalism*. Chicago, IL: University of Chicago Press.

Wallen, Jack. 2019. "8 Data Center Predictions for 2020." TechRepublic. December 15, 2019. https://www.techrepublic.com/article/8-data-center-predictions-for-2020/.

Walsh, Bryan. 2013. "The Surprisingly Large Energy Footprint of the Digital Economy." *TIME*, August 14, 2013. https://science.time.com/2013/08/14/power-drain-the-digital-cloud-is-using-more-energy-than-you-think/.

Weber, Max. 2012. *The Protestant Ethic and the Spirit of Capitalism*. London: Routledge.

Wells, Sarah. 2018. "The Challenges of Migrating 150+ Microservices to Kubernetes." Presented at the Kubecon, Copenhagen, May 2. https://www.youtube.com/watch?v=H06qrNmGqyE.

Winner, Langdon. 1980. "Do Artifacts Have Politics?" *Daedalus* 109 (1): 121–36.

Yuventi, Jumie, and Roshan Mehdizadeh. 2013. "A Critical Analysis of Power Usage Effectiveness and Its Use in Communicating Data Center Energy Consumption." *Energy and Buildings* 64 (September): 90–94. https://doi.org/10.1016/j.enbuild.2013.04.015.

Zaharia, Matei, Benjamin Hindman, Andy Konwinski, Ali Ghodsi, Anthony D. Joesph, Randy Katz, Scott Shenker, and Ion Stoica. 2011. "The Datacenter Needs an Operating System." In *Proceedings of the 3rd USENIX Conference on Hot Topics in Cloud Computing*, 17. HotCloud'11. Portland, OR: USENIX Association.

Zoellick, Jan Cornelius, and Arpita Bisht. 2018. "It's Not (All) about Efficiency: Powering and Organizing Technology from a Degrowth Perspective." *Journal of Cleaner Production*, Technology and Degrowth, 197 (October): 1787–99. https://doi.org/10.1016/j.jclepro.2017.03.234.

4   Resilience and Failure

On a normal Tuesday morning at Netflix, senior engineer Nora Jones sets up a new experiment. Normally, latency—the time taken for a user request to be returned by the server—hovers under the 20 millisecond mark. However, bringing up ChAP, their "chaos engineering" tool, Jones dials it all the way up to 600 milliseconds, a massive delay that might occur during a traffic spike, or when a user's internet connection was temporarily disrupted. Once configured, the experiment is run, inducing crashes and errors, and highlighting a number of vulnerabilities in existing services. Yet for Jones, this was assumed. Her job is about identifying the "chaos that's already inherent in the system, and being able to engineer around that" (Jones 2018).

Despite locating weaknesses, Jones does not send a patch request immediately. Instead, she meets with the development teams, pointing out these issues in order to "capture the learnings from vulnerabilities" (2018). She wants to know what went wrong from an information architecture point of view, but also what were the human assumptions that lead to this decision in the first place. Key for resiliency at the company is identifying the "culture" of non-resiliency, the intermingling of thought and practice that was too cavalier, too secure, or simply too misinformed. These employees failed to see failure as inevitable. Yet during the meeting, there is no blaming or rule-enforcing. After all, the goal of perfection, of resolving every issue and weeding out every error, is an impossible one. Instead, as Jones stresses (2019), "the goal is to push forward on a journey of resilience *through* the vulnerabilities we find."

Jones and her chaos engineering tool are one small example of a shift, a transformation not just in informational architectures, but in the broader paradigm of how systems of governance should best operate. This is a paradigm with a particular vision and significant stakes, a framework for how states and subjects should approach

DOI: 10.4324/9781003341185-4

crises that increasingly threaten lives and livelihoods. Drawing together emerging infrastructural technologies and practices with resilience and governance theories, this chapter examines that shift through the lens of the data center.

The argument proceeds section by section. "Reinforced Infrastructures" outlines how data centers have been traditionally understood as reinforced architectures capable of defending against any attack. However, this inefficient approach is increasingly being rethought. "From Reinforcement to Resiliency" sketches the historical evolution from a model of reinforcement to a more flexible, ecologically inspired model of resilience. "Resiliency through Failure Design" and "Resiliency through Autonomous Automation" demonstrate how this model of resilience is implemented in the data center through failure-by-design and automated adaptation. Finally, "Infrastructures as Operational Imaginaries" introduces the term operational imaginary to suggest that these infrastructures provide a broader blueprint for governance, a vision for the future that derives power from its materiality and functionality in the present.

These infrastructures operationalize key motifs of resilient-thinking, but also point beyond themselves, offering working models for coping with fundamental political and environmental uncertainty and suggesting how the contingency inherent to life might best be encountered, embraced, and adapted to. By remaining attentive to such infrastructures, we gain a more nuanced understanding of how resilience operates and what it seems to offer, critical insights into a mode of thought that has risen to become a dominant paradigm.

Reinforced Infrastructures

"Indestructible operations," stressed one data center engineer, "are the ultimate targets of all data centre designs" (Haag 2019). In this view, the data center is an impervious object, barricaded against threats, that can maintain operations while successfully repelling disasters, attacks, and failures. The goal is to keep going no matter what, an imperative that data center company Vertiv signaled with its new slogan: Continuity Architects. In the data center industry, the gold standard of high availability is "3 nines," or uptime of 99.9%. Indeed, the enterprise class data centers that underpin the operations of technology giants like Google, Facebook, China Mobile, and Aliyun must achieve uptime of 99.995%, a figure that equates to just 26.3 minutes of downtime over the course of an entire year (Colocation America 2019). Such high availability, the understanding goes, can only be achieved by doubling critical systems and locking out threats. Functionality is maintained through fortification.

In a 2017 paper, media scholar Tung-Hui Hu followed this framing. "Data centers," he suggested, should be "understood as a form of infrastructure designed to sustain itself at all costs" (Hu 2017, 85). Data has become a vital asset which must be secured against the ravages of the future. Indeed, Hu (2017, 85) suggests that "data centers offer a fantasy of indefinite preservation: there is a family resemblance between cold storage for data and cryopreservation." As a valuable asset, data becomes vulnerable to a whole range of potential threats, from natural disasters to nuclear war and cyberterrorism. Given these conditions, infrastructures become critical strongholds, safeguarding their contents by resisting the onslaught from the outside. Data centers, Hu (2017, 85) concludes, "embody the paranoid's architecture of internal security and external threat."

Driven by these anxieties, the architecture of the data center can certainly be understood as one which must reinforce itself against threats, whether real or imagined. First, data centers are reinforced against failure in the form of redundancy. Axiomatic in the industry is that single points of failure are unacceptable. Every primary critical system must be supported by other systems, preferably one that is physically or infrastructurally isolated from the first. This is the logic of N+1 redundancy, which ensures that operations continue without service interruption. In case of power failure, banks of uninterruptible power supplies (UPSs) provide backup electricity, while basement cooling plants ensure servers do not overheat. In fact, UPS systems are only a temporary measure while massive diesel generators are starting up. The MEGAPlus data center in Hong Kong, for instance, features multiple underground fuel tanks with a total capacity of 120,000 liters (SUNeVision 2019). Uptime Institute's Tier Classification System, an enormously influential rating in the industry, evaluates data centers primarily by their infrastructural redundancy. To qualify for Tier III and Tier IV, data centers must demonstrate their "operational sustainability" through systems that "have an effective life beyond the current IT requirement" (Uptime Institute 2018). A Tier IV design requires double the infrastructure of a Tier III design. Flagship data centers like Digital Realty, for example, feature 2N redundancy. Critical systems such as electricity are doubled in the form of "feeds from separate substations diversely routed to ground floor substations"

(Digital Realty 2017). From water to cooling to electricity, the perfectly redundant data center is designed from the beginning with far more resources than required to sustain it.

Second, data centers are reinforced against external threats. Exposure to natural threats such as fire, flood, or tsunami can be minimized by the choice of site location. In this regard, former Cold War bunkers such as Bahnhof Pionen in Sweden or the "nuke proof" Iron Mountain in the United States predominant in the minds of both the public and infrastructural scholars (Jakobsson and Stiernstedt 2012; Veel 2017). Yet on a more prosaic level, data center promotional literature often acknowledges the importance of the site, explaining why this particular location was chosen. A spec sheet for the flagship data center MEGAPlus, for instance, stresses that although it is on a peninsula in Hong Kong, it is on the far side, "away from the seafront" and "not in a flood zone" (SUNeVision 2019). Along with natural threats are human threats. At another data center, external measures like hydraulic bollards, security guards, and crash-proof barriers are designed to thwart vehicle attacks on the building itself, while internally, man traps, anti-tailgating devices, and two-factor authentication attempt to secure server rooms from unauthorized entry (Equinix 2015). If these features are designed to blend seamlessly into a contemporary office environment, they nevertheless continue the longstanding imperatives of military structures—to bunker down, to barricade, to defend. In this sense, data center infrastructures dovetail into broader discourses of security, which "saturate and militarize the tiniest details of everyday urban life" (Graham 2006, 61). The language of breach used in data center literature suggests a dangerous encroachment into a securitized zone. "The surrounding environment must be viewed holistically and watched proactively for threats and intrusions," states a white paper from data center power company APC: "Such threats include excessive server intake temperatures, water leaks, and unauthorized human access to the data center or inappropriate actions by personnel in the data center" (Cowan and Gaskins 2006). Whether natural or human threat, data centers are designed to avoid, thwart, and ultimately survive these attacks in order to continue operating.

Third, data centers are reinforced against time and change itself. Obsolescence, in the form of the data center that lacks the desired space or services, becomes a critical threat. The immense time and capital required to plan, design, and construct a data center means that data centers are major investments. Data centers are thus designed for the future, not the present. Electrical supplies in the megawatts are secured before the first server is even turned on. Cavernous empty server halls attempt to anticipate the next customer and their hyperscale needs. Indeed, in both electrical capacity and square footage, data centers are growing. "Only five years ago you felt a 250,000 sq ft building with 10MW was a lot. Now we may do a lease for 36MW for one client, and they'll take it in six rooms," observes one industry insider (Judge 2019). Amplifying the data center's infrastructural footprint aims to resist irrelevance, to be future proof. These sprawling hyperscale facilities attempt to not just match today's needs, but bolster themselves against tomorrow's. "The data center," asserts Elerding (2016), "is a nexus of wastefulness due to the infrastructural redundancy required to meet contemporary users' expectations—or anticipated expectations." In this sense, the overengineering typical of data centers is a form of temporal bulwarking, massively overdelivering in the present so as to maintain technical operations and business competitiveness in the future.

Taken together, such architectures of reinforcement suggest an indestructible data center and unstoppable functionality. The logics of cloud infrastructure, declare Jennifer Holt and Patrick Vonderau (2015, 205), "like nuclear power plants—are rooted in excess, redundancy, and contingency, governed by the looming specter of worst-case scenarios." If this description is not inaccurate, it follows a well-trodden path. Despite natural disasters, infrastructural collapse, or human antagonism, the data center—with its servers barricaded in a bunker-like architecture, secured by surveillance and sensor detection, and backed up by generators and uninterruptible power supplies—must remain operational. In this framing, unbroken operations are achieved by an unbreakable infrastructure.

Yet while this framing of reinforced architectures has merit, it fails to grasp recent shifts in data center infrastructures. The industry is beginning to realize that a culture that equates more safety with more infrastructure leads to a fundamental wastefulness (Miller 2019c). Data centers are over-engineered—bloated, energy-consumptive facilities that are both financially expensive and environmentally destructive. As researchers like Mel Hogan (2015) have demonstrated, these excessive infrastructures draw upon vast volumes of water and electricity, diverting increasingly scarce natural resources away from other uses in order to sustain their operations. But perhaps more subtly, there is a kind of inflexibility to such systems, a barricaded, lumbering power that remains impervious but also oblivious to the changes occurring around it. The model of reinforcement thus creates excessive systems, petrified processes, bulky designs—an infrastructural heaviness. "So much weight," suggests Orit Halpern (2017) "makes us dream of being plastic and light, mobile, modulatory, capable of bearing all these materialities while continuing to sustain the technical and economic fantasies of eternal growth and novel change." To follow this shift, the next section sketches a brief genealogy of resilience.

From Reinforcement to Resiliency

The architecture of reinforcement sketched in the previous section can be traced to the Cold War, where the threat of a possible thermonuclear strike initiated an infrastructure of anxiety. ARPANET, the network infrastructure that would form the basis of the later internet, emerges from this age of apprehension. In *Inventing the Internet*, Janet Abbate describes how engineer Paul Baran set out to design a "survivable communication system" that would be "built with the expectation of heavy damage" (1999, 10, 17). If one critical node in the network was struck by a nuclear attack, traffic would reroute around it, using alternate nodes to maintain connectivity. In this sense, paranoia became integrated as a de-facto network design schema, propagating in the form of carefully distanced nodes added over time. Exposure to danger would be diminished by highly redundant systems that could quickly return to their default operating conditions.

This Cold War notion of resiliency, underpinned by systems thinking, was about maintaining equilibrium. In this view, as Melinda Cooper and Jeremy Walker (2011, 146) note, a threat or adverse event disrupted the variables within a system, knocking them into higher or lower levels than normal. Resiliency, then, was the ability to return these integers rapidly to their operational defaults, to come back to a "steady state" as quickly as possible. In this framing, making systems more resilient meant anticipating exactly what kinds of threats they would undergo. Techniques such as scenario planning would play through an adverse event in meticulous detail, listing all of its possible effects and the specific measures that would be needed to overcome it (Kahn 1968; Mann 2004). Thus, if one aspect of this version of resiliency is the image of the backup generator, the other is the image of the flowchart diagram, with every contingency accounted for. Exposure to danger would be reduced by exhaustively defining it and preemptively implementing countermeasures.

However, the concept of resiliency would soon shift. In the 1970s, observe Cooper and Walker (2011, 146), this simplistic notion of resiliency began to be challenged by a more sophisticated ecological understanding. Ecologists such as CS Holling suggested that the former assumption—environments underwent cycles of stress, but always returned to their original or normal state—was fundamentally incorrect. Instead, environments were in a state of dynamic flux, and extreme events could leave them irrevocably altered. For Holling (1973, 17), resilience was "a measure of the ability of these systems to absorb changes of state variables, driving variables, and parameters, and still persist."

Resiliency thus drew upon its ecological roots to assert that life could ultimately not be secured. As David Chandler and Julian Reid explain (2016, 67), living systems could not wall themselves off from the threats inherent to life itself. Organisms needed to remain structurally open to the risk immanent within life. In fact, the most successful organisms not only survived such crises but also adapted to them, shifting them from a potential threat to an agent of productive transformation. Applying this biological insight to the sphere of governance initiates a fundamental shift in posture toward the uncertain exterior world. Once this understanding is taken up, Wakefield and Braun (2014, 5) point out, "crisis is no longer that which is to be warded off, eliminated, or overcome, but that which must be absorbed, attenuated, and survived." Resilience was not just an ability to bounce back, but to adapt to these new conditions and still thrive.

Moreover, contrary to the Cold War stance, resiliency was not about forecasting the precise nature of the next attack. Holling (1973, 21) stressed that this new ecological resilience was predicated not on the "assumption that future events are expected, but that they will be unexpected." There were too many possible variables to contend with, too many potential vectors of attack. Adverse events could never be entirely anticipated. Given these fundamentally uncertain conditions, the designer of resilient systems "does not require a precise capacity to predict the future, but only a qualitative capacity to devise systems that can absorb and accommodate future events in whatever unexpected form they may take" (Holling, 1973, 21).

Throughout the 1980s and 1990s, as Cooper and Walker (2011, 147) note, Holling's work on resiliency moved out from the narrow confines of ecological theory to encompass "societies and ecosystems as a total complex system." The concept has now found fertile homes in disciplines from climate science, to governmental planning, critical infrastructure protection, and even psychological development. Across these diverse fields, resiliency offers a common vocabulary of threat, adaptation and preparedness, and a pragmatic goal in the face of an incredibly complex and essentially antagonistic world—survive and thrive. Resilience, then, has proven broadly applicable, extending into an overarching diagram for governance and forming a set of imperatives for urban centers, infrastructures, and citizens alike. "Running through each design, plan, or experiment is not just the same presupposition ... but also the same problem: how to govern this totality" argue Wakefield and Braun (2014, 4): "Through what modes of arranging and ordering urban life might resilience be achieved? What is this life that is imagined, and how is it to be constructed?"

In *Resilience: The Governance of Complexity*, David Chandler takes up these questions, arguing that resilience has become the guiding force of governmentality. Life must be sustained against threat. Yet, threats emerge from a fundamentally complex world, one that can never entirely be tamed or corralled. For Chandler, then, the ascendance of governance-as-resilience is directly linked to the disenchantment with governance-as-control—a growing awareness of the limits of governments, of their historical inability to identify and avert threats, to adequately anticipate and control adversities. Complexity will always be overwhelming and fundamentally uncontrollable. Yet citizens, like systems, can be simultaneously strengthened—bolstered against upcoming adversity and unpredictable risk—and made more supple, able to cope with dynamism and successfully adapt to shifting conditions. For Chandler (2014, 65): "Resilience-thinking enables power to rule as the governance of life: enabling, empowering, facilitating and capacity-building."

Embedded within life and all its inherent contingency, resilient-thinking realizes its own limits, stressing instead on a pragmatic response: to manage rather than overcome complexity and risk. In this framework, Chandler asserts (2014, 65): "Life is the means and ends of governance with practice-based policy-making, self-reflexivity, feedback-loops, reflexive law-making and the inculcation of community capacities and resilience." Grand programs of authority wielded from above become supplanted by modest interventions from within. "Ruling 'through' rather than ruling 'over' implies a much flatter ontological relation between governing and being governed," notes Chandler (2014, 65). In this sense, governance becomes a diffuse network of services and micro-helps that the citizen can draw upon. Indeed, this scaffold of small supports recalls the "infra" in infrastructure. Rather than a top-down governance, this is a governance of under-among. In undergoing these shifts, the notion of resiliency itself emerges fundamentally changed. Superficially, of course, the discourse of resiliency in data centers never deviates from its cybernetic systems language and the maintenance of a steady state. In *Designing Risk in IT Infrastructure*, systems architect Daemon Behr asserts that in referring to resiliency, "we are referring to the change of state of a system from 'operable' to 'inoperable'" (2018, 33). For engineers, the resilient data center is one that remains functional in the face of adversity. The goal is to "ensure that data is consistent, applications are available, responsive and that there is allowance for multiple concurrent failures in every region without impact to users" (Behr 2018, 89).

However, drawing on its ecological influences, resiliency assumes that maintaining can only be achieved by constantly changing. As Holling suggested, infrastructure architects assume that future attacks can never entirely be planned for or anticipated. Threats to critical infrastructures are not just incessant, but incessantly shifting. For data center engineers, threat is always shapeshifting into exotic new forms: from the STUXNET worm designed to infect industrial computers to the Mariposa botnet (Maglaras et al. 2018) and on to more recent vectors such as the malware of GreyEnergy (Palmer 2019) and the ransomware of LockerGoga (Greenberg 2019). The specter of vulnerability reappears in new guises. Given this unpredictability, Behr admits: "You can never truly remove all risk, but you can understand the effects of every design decision" (2018, 35). Constantly evolving threats must be met by a mode of operation characterized by monitoring, reflectivity, adaptability, and learning. The incredibly high availability expected of data centers can only be attained through adaptation.

How is this new understanding of resilience enacted on an infrastructural level? Within the data center, the architectures of reinforcement discussed earlier by no means disappear. Threats are thwarted with security mechanisms such as gate controls, vehicle bollards, and mantraps, while operations are backed up with facilities like diesel generators or connections to a secondary electrical grid. However, a new set of features attempt to augment and even supplant these heavy architectures of reinforcement. The "prime directive" of uptime has traditionally been accomplished "through layers of redundant electrical infrastructure, including uninterruptible power supply (UPS) systems and emergency backup generators," writes data center analyst Rich Miller (2019c), "but cloud computing is bringing change to how companies approach uptime, introducing architectures that create resiliency using software and network connectivity." The next two sections thus explore how the traditional reinforcements core to data centers are supplemented by more supple architectures of resilience.

Resiliency through Failure Design

One key shift in resilient-thinking has been an approach to failure. If the mantra of modern infrastructure was that failure was unthinkable, the slogan of resilient infrastructure is that failure is inevitable. "Rather than promising the future understood in terms of progress and improvement, resilience infrastructure flips the temporality and politics of modern infrastructure," writes Stephanie Wakefield: "Instead, resilience assumes a future of inevitable and worsening crisis and seeks only to minimize its effects, adapting to changing conditions so as to keep existing socioeconomic conditions of liberal life the same (or perhaps more accurately, on life support)" (2018, 7). For data center architects, backup systems should certainly be arranged and maintained, but despite these efforts, failure can never be entirely preempted or prevented, only managed.

The Hystrix software library exemplifies this approach to failure. Developed originally by Netflix for its cloud services, Hystrix is now used by companies such as eBay and Capital One, and can be integrated with IBM Cloud and Amazon Web Services (Gopal 2015). On its developer page, Hystrix is described as a "latency and fault tolerance library designed to isolate points of access to remote systems, services and 3rd party libraries, stop cascading failure and enable resilience in complex distributed systems where failure is inevitable" (Netflix Engineering 2019). At a lay level, Hystrix can be explained with a simple scenario. On a day with unusually high traffic, such as Black Friday, a cloud company might be inundated with requests from users. These are all directed through their API, which acts as a front door for all requests. If one of the services comprising the API goes down, calls to this service generate an error. Because services are linked and dependent on one another, the error propagates, causing every other service to fail. User requests become stalled and are added to a queue, but never delivered. As a result, the queue becomes longer and longer, increasing server load and causing more users to experience delays and time-out errors. An unexpected failure in a single point produces a cascading failure at all points. To avoid this scenario, Hystrix provides cloud architectures with a virtual circuit breaker.[1] Programmers "wrap" a protected function call in a circuit breaker object, which constantly monitors itself for failures. Once a failure threshold is met, the circuit "breaks" or trips. Instead of inundating a failed service with more calls, calls stop being sent altogether. Moreover, the circuit breaker pattern allows developers to designate a series of next steps that will occur after this moment of failure. As an IBM developer page explains, such steps could be to "Fail silently," returning null, "Fail quickly," throwing an exception, or "Best Effort," returning a close approximation of the requested data.

Rather than rely on fail-safe systems, these next steps admit that failure will occur. Indeed, the circuit breaker pattern is a device for designing failure *into* critical systems. Rather than allowing hardware to max out, software is used to define low failure thresholds— to fail fast and early. Rather than allow failure to cascade, resulting in system-wide collapse, circuit breakers isolate a single function, limiting the fallout. And rather than failure triggering default system errors such as a time-out, circuit breakers let engineers construct custom workarounds specifically for this situation.

Hystrix thus attempts not just to account for failure, but to integrate failure itself into the design of a cloud service. In this sense, the unpredicted event of an electrical blackout, an internet outage, or a sudden surge of users is not treated as an anomaly, but as normality. As Director of Platform Engineering Ruslan Meshenberg (2014) stated: "It allows you to have control of what happens when things fail—not if, when." Indeed, Meshenberg suggests that engineering teams purposefully trigger failures during the day when the full support team is present, rather than improvising when they occur spontaneously in the middle of the night. In a presentation at the North American Network Operators group, engineering manager Josh Evan (2015) reiterated this approach, laying out Netflix's set of tools for purposefully injecting faults and forcing failures, stressing that other operators should follow suit. In actively internalizing contingency and programming with error, such tools embody one of the key concepts of resilient-thinking: danger cannot be held at arms length, but must be actively embraced.

Resiliency through Autonomous Automation

Along with designing in failure, the industry is now striving to transform the data center itself into a more autonomous unit. From standardization to self-monitoring, these seemingly diverse initiatives all aim to break down the barriers to automated resiliency. One hurdle, for instance, is the proprietary nature of data centers. Maintenance to custom hardware or electrical fit-outs requires calling out a data center engineer who can understand a particular configuration and make careful changes. In response, recent initiatives like Open19 have begun to designate a standardized hardware and software architecture. The Open19 specification rationalizes the server rack, transforming a cluster of proprietary components into a modular, universal kit. The goal is to essentially turn servers into plug and play devices. Cabling is moved to the back of the rack, enabling servers to be slotted straight into power ports; software then "autodetects it and auto-provisions it" (Branscombe 2018).

In this vision, rather than the time delay and cost incurred by having a qualified technician visit the site, a server could be replaced by anyone. Indeed, one of the technical leads on the project envisions "a robotic hand that can remove a faulty server and insert a replacement, much like a tape robot changing tapes in digital tape archives today" (Branscombe 2018). If maintenance is key to remaining operational, the aim is to reduce reliance on human intervention, to automate that maintenance as much as possible. As the developer (Branscombe 2018) explains: "standardization, along with hardware isolation inside the rack, self-monitoring, and self-healing provisioning systems, are all pieces of the puzzle in creating fully automated, or 'lights-out' data centers."

The dream of the lights-out data center is continuous operation supported through automation. For the data center industry, the current dependency on qualified human labor is considered a weakness. The industry has a major employment problem, struggling to attract and retain qualified personnel. It's very hard to find specialists in security, networking, and even in data center construction. Moreover, the expected explosion of micro and edge data centers is expected to overwhelm the already nominal numbers of staff at companies. "There is a real risk that the level of activity causes burnout on your network team," stated one industry insider (Miller 2019a): "We need to invest in automation to get time back."

Given this lack of labor, the lights-out data center thus seeks to remove the final concession to human engineers and their meat eye needs—light to see what they're doing. The key point here is that resilient-thinking reframes the point of weakness. The vulnerability is *not* the uncertainty and threats that emerge from the outside, but the over-reliance on an all-too-human response, an individual who can only be in one place at a time, who can make mistakes, and who must be trained, paid, and placed on-call. Infrastructures thus aim to embody the vision of an autonomous form of machinic life, one that can predict its own maintenance, diagnose its own errors, and implement its own recovery plan. Decoupled from human labor, the data center becomes ostensibly self-sustaining. It epitomizes the dream of capital itself, which, as Rita Raley reminds us, is seen as being "given to mutation and flexibility, not to self-destruction, but to autotelic reproduction and regeneration" (2009, 134). In this sense, the pitch dark data center embodies the longstanding dream of total automation, but accomplishes it through flexibility rather than invulnerability.

Along with standardization, predictive maintenance is also seen as a promising path in rendering the data center more autonomous. Rather than waiting until hardware breaks to replace it, or alternatively, defining a set schedule of maintenance which could be too frequent, predictive maintenance seeks to optimize replacement times using data from a device's lifecycle: temperature, hours operating, model characteristics, and so on. Such initiatives are only just underway. Currently, some companies are "offering heavily supervised machine learning algorithms" that are only available for their particular product; however, "real benefits in this space will come when a firm obtains a critical mass of data that aligns equipment types, power usage, performance, incident and maintenance data" (Miller 2019b).

Whether or not such a moment will ever arrive is arguable. However the key point here is that predictive maintenance takes a formerly awkward or unspoken aspect of systems—their vulnerability to wear and tear—and actively internalizes it. Indeed, the volumes of data required for robust machine learning models suggest that this inspection of internal failure will need to not only be wide ranging, taking into account various models across dozens of data centers, but also meticulous in its attention to detail. From deterioration to overheating and errors, failure in all of its facets will need to be obsessively documented. The more fine grained the analysis of failure can become, the more accurate predictive maintenance can be. If a reinforced data center strives to stave off general obsolescence, a resilient data center stresses that hardware obsolescence must be deeply understood and integrated as a feature of the system.

Infrastructures as Operational Imaginaries

Data centers thus demonstrate two key concepts of resilience. Hystrix and similar error injection strategies embody the *embrace of failure*. Rather than relying on the reinforced architectures of modernity, which claim to hold threats at bay, these tools assume that failure is unavoidable. It is not a question of if, but when. Implementing resilience means accepting this constant exposure. Developers model this embrace by developing for error, consciously and repeatedly exposing a system to vulnerabilities and actively "designing in" latency, disaster, and outages. Alongside this, new initiatives of automated maintenance epitomize the mantra of *learning from failure*. In the world of resilient-thinking, uncertainty is the new normal, a set of conditions that privilege adaptation above all. The goal is not to return to a default state as quickly as possible, but to reflect on each crisis, internalizing the necessary adjustments and emerging stronger and more supple. Data centers seek to monitor each new threat and meticulously register each hardware or software failure. Machine learning initiatives churn over these collected failures in search of insights, developing more robust models better able to self-monitor and self-heal.

What are the stakes of such shifts within data center architectures? Certainly, infrastructures are always political in that they structure the immediate possibilities available to the people and things that surround them. Infrastructures both enable and disable particular kinds of action, Graham and McFarlane (2015, 33) suggest, and thus are forms of "(attempted) control, power and exclusion." As life becomes conducted in and through informational systems, data centers move beyond utilities to become critical gatekeepers. Data centers become mediators for a whole array of public and private practices, facilitating financial transactions, reconfiguring forms of labor through platforms, extracting value through machine learning, and underpinning critical aspects of government surveillance regimes (Munn 2018). In storing, processing, and distributing that information in particular ways, data centers funnel value and capital to some while disregarding others, maintaining asymmetric power structures. By enabling certain ways of being and doing while making others impossible or unthinkable, infrastructures shape the politics of the everyday.

One of the strengths of infrastructure studies has been its ability to clearly demonstrate this critical role that infrastructure plays in *underpinning* forms of contemporary life. From transport networks in Tokyo (Fisch 2018) to mobile communications in India (Doron and Jeffrey 2013), and electricity blackouts in America (Nye 2010), these studies show how infrastructures provide crucial functionality for everyday existence, sustaining human and non-human activity at a variety of levels. Yet, more emphasis could be placed on the role of infrastructures in *prototyping* forms of future life. Infrastructures are functional mockups where concepts can be integrated and operationalized, providing models that shape important discussions and influence key decisions. In this sense, infrastructures should also be understood as *operational imaginaries*—as systems that powerfully suggest a set of future possibilities by enacting them concretely in the present.

Infrastructures are by definition operational, a dependability that quickly moves them from spectacular technology to everyday utility, from the novel to the banal. Yet, it is precisely this operational quality that makes their imaginaries of resilient life more powerful. Infrastructures are not nebulous fantasies but functional realities, anchored in cables and copper, switchgear and server racks. Infrastructures are pipes, not pipe dreams. As Brian Larkin (2018, 188) suggests: "Infrastructures are formal expressions of experience, vehicles whereby that experience is made palpably real to people." If infrastructures draw upon the concept of resilience, they also contribute back to it, legitimating its promise through their hard materiality and pragmatic functionalism. "Infrastructures never just supply electricity, water, or gas," argues Larkin (2018, 189), "they implicate the very definition of the community, its possible futures, and its relation to the state." Infrastructures point beyond themselves, implying that the same operational logics deployed within hardware stacks, software suites, and best practice procedures might be productively applied to the governance of other things.

Perhaps one of the most enticing qualities of infrastructure for its proponents is its technical approach to life. It is unsurprising that this approach, in bracketing out much of this messiness of the social and epistemological, would be appealing to regimes of governance. Whether sustaining access to data against a constant barrage of threats or sustaining citizens against a mounting series of political and environmental crises, the solution is to develop a more comprehensive, smart, and supple system. As Brad Evans and Julian Reid (2015, 18) observe, "infrastructure becomes 'critical' to the understanding of living systems," to the "discourses and practices of securitization, especially in global cities." Liberal governance is a system that maintains the life-capacities of its subjects first by embracing contingency and uncertainty: investigating internal vulnerabilities, constantly monitoring for new threats, and incessantly seeking out those unknown unknowns. After identifying these vulnerabilities, the resilient system must adapt to them: updating its protocols, integrating new routines, and encoding a more robust set of operations and solutions to buffer itself against the threats it will inevitably face in the future. Indeed, the most positive variations of resilient-thinking see uncertainty and chaos as a crucible for creativity, a chance to respond to existential threats with innovative new technical solutions.

Based on this technical approach, infrastructure seems to hold out the promise of a pragmatic internal program. Key for resilient-thinking is the assumption that the world is essentially broken and will remain broken. It is a lost cause, one that is too vast, too complex, too shot through with catastrophes of all kinds. As Evans and Reid (2015, 38) stress, it is "insecure by design." Altering these broader systemic conditions, whether political, social, or environmental, is fundamentally impossible, a grand task doomed to failure. The uncertainty and precarity swirling "out there" will persist and constantly reappear in unpredictable new forms. Instead, the remit of governance is ratcheted down to something far more modest and more manageable. All one can do is to improve your own system, implementing a set of internal capacities and mobilizing a set of local strategies. In the face of the overwhelming and the ungovernable, operational imaginaries offer a set of action points and indicators, a concrete series of best practices and next steps. The task at hand is not to change the world, but to integrate a set of buffers and responses into this nation-state, this city, this subject.

Thus, if infrastructure is an "operating system for shaping the city," as Keller Easterling (2016, 10) suggested, it also suggests an operating system for shaping the territory, a means of reestablishing some kind of successful order by narrowing governance down from grand visions of improvement to a pragmatic focus on basic functionality. Resilient infrastructures are successful implementations of a broader political vision in which crises are not averted, but adapted to. They provide real-world demonstrations showing how systems might "anticipate the uncertain" through "networked infrastructure that has itself automated emergence and change as regular and manageable processes" (Halpern et al. 2013, 295). In this sense, they embody a vision of a necessarily vulnerable future where instability becomes a default operating condition. By designing in failure and integrating adaptability into their architectures, data centers act as functional prototypes for new forms of governance. In working, they demonstrate that resilient-thinking can and will work.

Modeled by functional infrastructure, resilience broadens into an imaginary, a blueprint for how to survive and thrive in a world permeated by ungovernable uncertainty. Whether coming in the form of natural disasters or political upheavals, cities can never reinforce themselves enough to ensure their invulnerability. Instead, as Orit Halpern (2017) suggests: "Resilience, now married to infrastructures of ubiquitous computing and logistics, becomes the dominant method for engaging with possible urban collapse (and also the collapse of more *sui generis* infrastructures of transport, energy grids, financial systems, etc)." In this imaginary, resilient cities can absorb the financial shocks caused by volatile global markets and the environmental shocks caused by an increasingly precarious planetary ecosystem. Infrastructures provide the current means to do this, but also the model for how future uncertainty might best be approached. In doing so, they fulfill a testbed function, providing a "study into the possible ways modern digital technologies change the way we *will* inhabit our cities and the means by which these technologies *will* change our perception and experience of urban reality" (Halpern et al. 2013, 292).

Similarly for the subject, bunkering herself in will not suffice. Individual architectures of reinforcement will be overwhelmed by some new life event, some unforeseen incursion. As AbdouMaliq Simone (2015, 123) observes, there will always be "contingencies that one could not quite get a handle on. From this perspective, then, everything becomes insufficient." Given these turbulent conditions, the contemporary subject must constantly evolve, developing new strategies of living before the old tactics stop working entirely. Like informational infrastructures, subjects must remain open to uncertainty and see it as an opportunity—both embracing and learning from failure. In this imaginary, resilient subjects can soak up the fallout of neoliberalization, adopting coping mechanisms and self-management strategies in order to function without the social safety nets that once supported them.

Data center infrastructures provide a lens for understanding the rise of resilience-thinking, for grasping the pragmatism and promise of resilience as approach. Data centers have typically been understood as indestructible infrastructures that maintain operations while keeping threats at bay. Data centers certainly attempt to reinforce themselves against environmental catastrophes, human intrusions, and the obsolescence that time itself threatens. Yet, data centers have also begun to integrate an ecological understanding of resilience. Unable to anticipate every threat and lock-out every contingency, resilient infrastructures strive to "design in" failure, monitor their own maintenance, and flexibly adapt to new threats, internalizing and adapt to changes. In rendering this resilience functional and operational, infrastructures contribute to an imaginary of resilient-thinking that has broadened to become a framework for the governance of life itself. In enacting resilience in the present, they anticipate possible futures; in modeling it now, they shape debates about the possibilities to come.

Note

1 The circuit breaker pattern was popularized by Michael Nygard in his 2007 book *Release It!* focused on "reducing system fragility" and creating applications that can withstand "harsh realities." Michael Nygard, *Release It!: Design and Deploy Production-Ready Software*, (Raleigh, NC: Pragmatic Bookshelf, 2007).

References

Abbate, Janet. 1999. *Inventing the Internet*. Cambridge, MA: MIT Press.

Behr, Daemon. 2018. *Designing Risk in IT Infrastructure*. IT Architect Series. Morrisville, NC: IT Architect.

Branscombe, Mary. 2018. "Why Open19 Is Being Designed as an Edge Data Center Standard." Data Center Knowledge. November 29, 2018. https://www.datacenterknowledge.com/edge-computing/why-open19-being-designed-edge-data-center-standard.

Chandler, David. 2014. *Resilience: The Governance of Complexity*. Critical Issues in Global Politics. New York: Routledge.

Chandler, David, and Julian Reid. 2016. *The Neoliberal Subject: Resilience, Adaptation and Vulnerability*. London; New York: Rowman & Littlefield International.

Colocation America. 2019. "Data Center Tier Rating Breakdown." Colocation America. February 14, 2019. https://www.colocationamerica.com/data-center/tier-standards-overview.htm.

Cowan, Christian, and Chris Gaskins. 2006. *Monitoring Physical Threats in the Data Center*. West Kingston, RI: American Power Conversion.

Digital Realty. 2017. "Digital Tseung Kwan O." https://go.digitalrealty.com/33-chun-choi-hongkong-BR?_ga=2.248024386.472017452. 1559081483-1163340322.1559081483.

Doron, Assa, and Robin Jeffrey. 2013. *The Great Indian Phone Book: How the Cheap Cell Phone Changes Business, Politics, and Daily Life.* Cambridge, MA: Harvard University Press.

Easterling, Keller. 2016. *Extrastatecraft: The Power of Infrastructure Space.* London: Verso.

Elerding, Carolyn. 2016. "The Materiality of the Digital: Petro-Enlightenment and the Aesthetics of Invisibility." *Postmodern Culture; Baltimore* 26 (2). http://search.proquest.com/docview/1844103389/abstract/849CE404D57B4730PQ/1.

Equinix. 2015. *IBX® Singapore 3 (SG3) Data Center Tour.* https://www.youtube.com/watch?v=AnDz9Clzs8k.

Evans, Brad, and Julian Reid. 2014. *Resilient Life: The Art of Living Dangerously.* Cambridge: Polity.

Evans, Josh. 2015. "Embracing Failure: Fault Injection and Service Resilience at Netflix." Presented at the North American Network Operators Group (NANOG) 61, Bellevue, WA, August 1. https://jturgasen.github.io/2015/08/01/tech-takeaway-021-embracing-failure-fault-injection-and-service-resilience-at-netflix-by-josh-evans.

Fisch, Michael. 2018. *An Anthropology of the Machine: Tokyo's Commuter Train Network.* Chicago, IL; London: The University of Chicago Press.

Garber, Kent. 2009. "The Internet's Hidden Energy Hogs: Data Servers." *US News & World Report*, March 24, 2009. https://www.usnews.com/news/energy/articles/2009/03/24/the-internets-hidden-energy-hogs-data-servers.

Gopal, Senthilkumar. 2015. "Application Resiliency Using Netflix Hystrix." EBay Tech Blogs. September 8, 2015. https://www.ebayinc.com/stories/blogs/tech/application-resiliency-using-netflix-hystrix/.

Graham, Stephen. 2006. "Urban Metabolism as Target: Contemporary War as Forced Demodernization." In *In the Nature of Cities*, edited by N. C. Heynen, M. Kaika, and E. Swyngedouw, 260–80. London: Routledge.

Graham, Stephen, and Colin McFarlane. 2015. "Introduction." In *Infrastructural Lives: Urban Infrastructure in Context*, edited by Stephen Graham and Colin McFarlane, 1–14. London: Routledge.

Greenberg, Andy. 2019. "A Guide to LockerGoga, the Ransomware Crippling Industrial Firms." *Wired*, March 25, 2019. https://www.wired.com/story/lockergoga-ransomware-crippling-industrial-firms/.

Haag, Wolfgang. 2019. "Credo." Data Centre Facilities. April 18, 2019. https://www.dwh-engineers.de/credo/.

Halpern, Orit, Jesse LeCavalier, Nerea Calvillo, and Wolfgang Pietsch. 2013. "Test-Bed Urbanism." *Public Culture* 25 (2 70): 272–306. https://doi.org/10.1215/08992363-2020602.

Halpern, Orit. 2017. "Hopeful Resilience." E-Flux Architecture. April 19, 2017. https://www.e-flux.com/architecture/accumulation/96421/hopeful-resilience/.

Hogan, Mél. 2015. "Data Flows and Water Woes: The Utah Data Center." *Big Data & Society* 2 (2): 205395171559242. https://doi.org/10.1177/2053951715592429.

Holling, C. S. 1973. "Resilience and Stability of Ecological Systems." *Annual Review of Ecology and Systematics* 4: 1–23.

Holt, Jennifer, and Patrick Vonderau. 2015. "'Where the Internet Lives': Data Centers as Cloud Infrastructure." In *Signal Traffic: Critical Studies of Media Infrastructures*, edited by Lisa Parks and Nicole Starosielski, 175–229. Chicago: University of Illinois Press.

Hu, Tung-Hui. 2017. "Black Boxes and Green Lights: Media, Infrastructure, and the Future at Any Cost." *English Language Notes* 55 (1–2): 81–88. https://doi.org/10.1215/00138282-55.1-2.81.

Jakobsson, Peter, and Fredrik Stiernstedt. 2012. "Time, Space and Clouds of Information: Data Centre Discourse and the Meaning of Durability." In *Cultural Technologies*, edited by Göran Bolin. New York: Routledge. https://doi.org/10.4324/9780203117354-14.

Jones, Nora. 2018. "Chaos Engineering: A Step Towards Resilience." Presented at the REdeploy 2018, San Francisco, August 17. https://www.youtube.com/watch?time_continue=40&v=qyzymLlj9ag.

———. 2019. "Chaos Engineering Traps." *Medium*. April 9, 2019. https://medium.com/@njones_18523/chaos-engineering-traps-e3486c526059.

Judge, Peter. 2019. "How Webscale Is Swallowing Colo." *Data Center Dynamics*. May 17, 2019. https://www.datacenterdynamics.com/analysis/how-webscale-swallowing-colo/.

Kahn, Herman. 1968. *On Escalation: Metaphors and Scenarios*. Baltimore, MD: Penguin Books.

Larkin, Brian. 2018. "Promising Forms: The Political Aesthetics of Infrastructure." In *The Promise of Infrastructure*, edited by Nikhil Anand, Akhil Gupta, and Hannah Appel, 175–202. Durham, NC: Duke University Press.

Maglaras, Leandros A., Ki-Hyung Kim, Helge Janicke, Mohamed Amine Ferrag, Stylianos Rallis, Pavlina Fragkou, Athanasios Maglaras, and Tiago J. Cruz. 2018. "Cyber Security of Critical Infrastructures." *ICT Express*, SI: CI & Smart Grid Cyber Security, 4 (1): 42–45. https://doi.org/10.1016/j.icte.2018.02.001.

Mann, James. 2004. "The Armageddon Plan." *The Atlantic*, March 1, 2004. https://www.theatlantic.com/magazine/archive/2004/03/the-armageddon-plan/302902/.

Meshenberg, Ruslan. 2014. "How Netflix's Open Source Tools Help Accelerate & Scale Services." Presented at the AWS re:Invent, Las Vegas, November 12. https://www.youtube.com/watch?v=p7ysHhs5hl0.

Miller, Rich. 2019a. "The Eight Trends That Will Shape the Data Center Industry in 2019." *Data Center Frontier* (blog). January 4, 2019. https://datacenterfrontier.com/the-eight-trends-that-will-shape-the-data-center-industry-in-2019/.

————. 2019b. "What's Next for AI in Data Center Automation?" *Data Center Frontier* (blog). March 20, 2019. https://datacenterfrontier.com/whats-next-for-ai-in-data-center-automation/.

————. 2019c. "Rethinking Redundancy: Is Culture Part of the Problem?" *Data Center Frontier* (blog). May 22, 2019. https://datacenterfrontier.com/rethinking-redundancy-is-culture-part-of-the-problem/.

Munn, Luke. 2018. *Ferocious Logics: Unmaking the Algorithm*. Lüneburg: Meson Press.

Netflix Engineering. (2012) 2019. *Hystrix* (version 1.5.18). Java. Netflix, Inc. https://github.com/Netflix/Hystrix.

Nye, David E. 2010. *When the Lights Went out: A History of Blackouts in America*. Cambridge, MA: MIT Press.

Nygard, Michael. 2007. *Release It!: Design and Deploy Production-Ready Software*. Raleigh, NC: Pragmatic Bookshelf.

Palmer, Danny. 2018. "GreyEnergy: New Malware Campaign Targets Critical Infrastructure Companies." ZDNet. Accessed June 18, 2019. https://www.zdnet.com/article/greyenergy-new-malware-campaign-targets-critical-infrastructure-companies/.

Raley, Rita. 2009. *Tactical Media*. Minneapolis: University of Minnesota Press.

Simone, AbdouMaliq. 2015. "Relational Infrastructures in Postcolonial Urban Worlds." In *Infrastructural Lives : Urban Infrastructure in Context*, edited by Stephen Graham and Colin McFarlane. London: Routledge.

SUNeVision. 2019. "MEGAPlus Data Sheet." https://www.iadvantage.net/images/pdf/MEGAPlus_DataSheet.pdf.

Uptime Institute. 2018. "Tier Classification System." May 21, 2018. https://uptimeinstitute.com/tiers.

Veel, Kristin. 2017. "Uncertain Architectures: Performing Shelter and Exposure." *Imaginations Journal* 8 (2): 30–41.

Wakefield, Stephanie. 2018. "Infrastructures of Liberal Life: From Modernity and Progress to Resilience and Ruins." *Geography Compass* 12 (7): 1–14.

Wakefield, Stephanie, and Bruce Braun. 2014. "Governing the Resilient City." *Environment and Planning D: Society and Space* 32 (1): 4–11.

Walker, Jeremy, and Melinda Cooper. 2011. "Genealogies of Resilience: From Systems Ecology to the Political Economy of Crisis Adaptation." *Security Dialogue* 42 (2): 143–60. https://doi.org/10.1177/0967010611399616.

5 Epilogue
Alternative Infrastructures

What should an infrastructure do? What makes one infrastructure better than another? And what do we mean by "better" anyway? As this book has shown, the values attached to and performed by infrastructures are typically utilitarian, obsessed with delivery and efficiency. Yet, these axioms, while firmly entrenched, are not the only ones that might be upheld. In this epilogue, I take a look at alternative infrastructures, considering different ways of structuring knowledge, approaching time, connecting people, and organizing labor. For this alternate canon of infrastructure, I largely leave behind infrastructure as it is—moving beyond computer science papers and software engineering case studies—and instead look to infrastructure as it might be, turning to cultural studies, artistic research, and indigenous software for speculative new models.

For Judith Butler (2015, 20), the demand for infrastructure is the demand for a "certain kind of inhabitable ground." In allowing us to do things—to store and retrieve medical knowledge, to send a message to a loved one, to buy an essential item online, or simply to obtain a glass of drinkable water—infrastructures contribute toward this inhabitable ground. They are the scaffolding that we rely on in countless small ways, the unseen structures that sustain ourselves and the people around us. And yet all too easily, as Butler (2015, 21) notes, this "dependency on infrastructure can also become subjugation." Infrastructures can be taken up and used in ways that restrict agency, that remove rights and opportunities. They can be calibrated to privilege some groups while suppressing others. Indeed, data infrastructures allow this calibration to become particularly fine-grained and flexible, with new rules and logics established as rapidly as a software update. Or infrastructures can be designed from the very beginning as tools of oppression. For Butler (2015, 20), these kinds of infrastructures contribute to the "decimation of livable life." This is why the "demand is not for

DOI: 10.4324/9781003341185-5

all kinds of infrastructure," but rather for systems, processes, and material forms that contribute meaningfully to the care of those around us—to making life more bearable, more endurable.

What, then, is our demand? What kind of infrastructures do we want? This is a fundamental or even basic question but one that infrastructures largely manage to avoid. As this book has showed, the triumph of infrastructure has been to steer discourse away from these "softer" questions of sociality and equality, and toward the "harder" facts of economy and utility. In a keynote lecture for *Former West*, curator Irit Rogoff (2013) notes "the degree to which infrastructure is deployed as either pure instrumentality or as a comforting panacea of assured Western standards of efficiency, communication, mobility, and subservience to economist arguments is truly alarming." In this instrumental framing, what matters is whether infrastructures function or not, whether they perform their task competently and consistently. Do they match their key performance indicators? Do they fulfill the program of delivery? Do they materialize the vision that was laid out to investors and the public? In essence, do they do what they promised they would do: do they work?

This utilitarian understanding produces a kind of hyper-reflexivity, where infrastructures look inward to justify themselves. This is a self-enclosed system, where an infrastructure's own operations—utility, speed, efficiency—are the only values that matter. The world, and more specifically competing groups with competing visions about how the world should work, is carefully bracketed off. This obsession with the instrumental produces a blinkered focus on acceleration and optimization. It matters not what is being done, only that it is being done faster and "better." But as F. G. Jünger (1990, 70) observes, this single-minded focus evades the key question: To what end? What is the purpose of these infrastructures? What are they accomplishing, and whom does it serve?

If an infrastructure can achieve a certain baseline operating standard, then it goes unquestioned. As the saying goes: if it ain't broke, don't fix it. But this preoccupation with operations—how something is being done—avoids the much broader and messier question of motivation—what is being done and why. Even if infrastructures work flawlessly—or precisely *because* they work flawlessly—they can be potent mechanisms for restricting rights and inhibiting freedoms, for maintaining racialized and gendered subjects, or even just for upholding mediocre "solutions" when other possibilities—more communal, more equitable, more radical—are readily available. As Rogoff (2013) observes, when we "congratulate ourselves on having an infrastructure—functioning institutions, systems of classification and categorization, archives and traditions and professional training for these, funding and educational pathways, excellence criteria ... we forget the degree to which these have become protocols that bind and confine us in their demand to be conserved." The danger of functional infrastructure, with its meticulous engineering of form and function, its immaculate choreography of tasks and gestures, is that it leaves us spellbound, blinded to other possibilities. Or perhaps for the disillusioned postmodern subject, the reaction is not so much awe as a passive acceptance that this is the way things work. But whether through technofetishism or fatalism, the result is an erasure of other options. Other ways of structuring society, of organizing knowledge, of connecting people and things, are successfully banished. There is no alternative.

Infrastructures always have a double-edged quality, supporting particular ways of being and thinking while inhibiting others. For philosopher of technology Gernot Böhme, it's clear that informational and technical infrastructures have the power to shape social and political life. Böhme sees these technical infrastructures as embodiments of Foucault's dispositif, a conditioning factor that both enables and disables certain types of activities and relations. Because of this deep structural influence, Böhme (2012, 7) asserts that "our society's existing technical infrastructure determines what is socially possible today." In their *Unbuilding Infrastructure* reader, Susannah Haslam and Tom Clark (2019, 3) echo this argument, suggesting that infrastructure is a technical structure that has social, material, and mediating qualities; these inherent qualities create a "ground on which activity takes place," establishing conditions "in which certain activities are possible and others are not."

"Is there a potential to think this model of efficient delivery critically?" asks Rogoff (2013). Infrastructure has been so thoroughly captured, so meticulously stripped of any political trace, that even to ask this question seems strangely awkward or out of place, a kind of secular blasphemy. To ask this question is to question progress itself, to open up a precarious line of thought that threatens to destabilize the systems that we take for granted in contemporary life. And yet this is precisely the question that this book posed, the question we need to ask and keep asking. One way to think infrastructures critically is to use them critically, employing them in alternative ways, a strategy that the next section explores.

Counter-Using Infrastructures

Infrastructures are constructed for a particular set of use cases. From its conception, the creators of an infrastructure—designers, developers, engineers—have envisaged that it will be used in a certain way. This is the program for an infrastructure. By embodying a set of technical requirements—speed, efficiency, power—this infrastructure will support a certain set of activities. These activities have been anticipated, catered for, carefully considered, and so infrastructure will excel at performing them. Used in their intended way, infrastructures render these activities seamless and second-nature. There is a kind of ordinariness to this activity, a taken-for-granted quality: of course the electricity works, of course the file sends, of course the data was stored. Used in this way, infrastructure becomes banal or even boring, dropping into the background. It is this dynamic which gives infrastructure its invisible quality. When used "properly" and frequently, infrastructures become hidden in plain sight.

But this doesn't preclude infrastructures from being used in other ways. Infrastructures can be taken up for other programs; they can be employed for other purposes. Infrastructures are ambidextrous. To grasp this flexibility, it's useful to turn to Keller Easterling and her notion of disposition. For Easterling, infrastructures come with a propensity, a tendency, much as a ball on a slope has a propensity to roll down it. Within this disposition, there are certainly "well-rehearsed sequences of code" (Easterling 2016, 131) uses and routines that have been repeated time and time again. And yet dispositions can never be entirely codified and cataloged. There are always novel ways to leverage an infrastructure, use cases that were never anticipated or accounted for. Levy Bryant (2014, 24) makes the same point when he suggests that machines are always "pluripotent." The particular way in which one machine is instrumentalized by another does not exhaust all it can do. Machines always have latent capacities or abilities that are not being drawn upon. Infrastructure, like any system, contains discrepancies between the total affordances of its constitutive objects and those which are utilized. In other words, there is a gap between an object's potential and how it is put-to-use. Andrew Feenberg (2008, 114) calls this gap the margin of maneuver, a margin "required for implementation in conformity with the dominant technical code, but also containing potentials incompatible with that code. Successful administration today consists in suppressing those dangerous potentials in the preservation of operational autonomy." Networks are one example of this unintended use. Networks came attached to a certain vision of their use. Because the network form is decentralized—an array of distributed servers that can redirect data flows whenever one node goes down—they were attended by a promise of political and communicational decentralization. No longer would we need to rely on centralized gatekeepers and media monopolies. Now everyone could be their own node, produce their own media, and communicate on their own terms. And yet the reality ended up differently. As Easterling (2018, 128) notes, at certain junctures, networks have ended up producing highly "constricting monopolies, whether scattered or centralized." The "walled gardens" created by contemporary tech titans demonstrate, somewhat perversely, the centralizing power of a decentralized infrastructure. This is just one way, in the words of Alexander Galloway (2004), that "control exists after decentralization."

However, even here there is a kind of elasticity, a suppleness, to such infrastructures. We might think, for instance, of how social media is often leveraged by progressive and protest movements to raise awareness and mobilize support to their cause. To be sure, scholars have long debated exactly how significant social media was to uprisings such as the Arab Spring. But the exact degree of influence is less important than the fundamental flexibility of these sociotechnical systems. Features designed to soak up attention and keep users on their phones can also be used to push citizens out onto the streets. Metrics with a tendency to perpetuate self-interest can also be useful for mobilizing a collective movement. A platform that has long maintained a hands-off stance to regulation and politics can be leveraged explicitly for political struggle. "Some of the most consequential political outcomes of infrastructure space remain undeclared in the dominant stories that portray them," asserts Easterling (2018, 129); they possess "some other agency or capacity" that has escaped detection.

These examples suggest that the uses of infrastructure can never be entirely mapped out. More sharply, they suggest that political possibility can never be entirely stripped out of infrastructure. Infrastructure, as this book has repeatedly shown, always purports to be apolitical, carrier-neutral, agnostic about the wider world and its messy mix of stakeholders and claims to power. And yet we know that this apolitical appearance is a fantasy; that infrastructures, in establishing the conditions for certain practices and certain people, are always-already political. Counter-uses of infrastructure, then, only make this truth overt, explicit. They stress that infrastructures used to uphold political power can also be used to subvert it, that systems that reinforce existing hegemonies may also be exploited to tear them down. As Easterling (2016, 134) stresses, we can always uncover "accidental, covert, or stubborn forms of power-political chemistries ... hiding in the folds of infrastructure space."

Decolonizing Infrastructure

For an example of an alternative infrastructure, we can turn to Te Hiku Media, a small non-profit media organization based at the northern tip of Aotearoa New Zealand. In 2018, Te Hiku ran a competition inviting its radio listeners to record themselves speaking Te Reo Māori, the language of the indigenous Māori people, and send it to them. As journalist Donavyn Coffey (2018) documents, Te Hiku were quickly overwhelmed by responses, receiving over 300 hours of annotated audio in a matter of weeks. While 320 hours is not a large dataset compared to other language repositories, it was enough to build an initial speech-to-text engine with a minimal error rate. This material will also form the basis for automated speech recognition, mobile applications, and other digital tools for the indigenous language.

To understand what these tools and data represent, we need to grasp the attempt to attack and erase the Māori language. Throughout the 19th and 20th centuries, children could be beaten, caned, or otherwise punished for speaking Te Reo in school (Neilson 2020). They learned that their native tongue was something to be ashamed of, to be kept at home or abandoned altogether. This whakamā or shame was internalized by that generation, who steered their children away from Te Reo so they wouldn't have to experience the same feelings. Children were instead forced to learn and speak English. This policy was only exacerbated by others such as urbanization and policies like "pepper potting" where Māori were housed with non-Māori. Together, these moves led to a significant decline in the language between 1920 and 1960 (Higgins and Keane 2015). These shifts were not simply about a preferred language, but about a more fundamental form of cultural assimilation. While initiatives over the last 50 years like Te Reo in schools and Māori language week signal a change in attitude, they only begin to remedy the long-term damage to language and culture that has been done. The same pattern can be seen all around the globe. The UN

Forum on Indigenous Issues (2018) estimates that one indigenous language dies every two weeks, and that by 2100, half of the world's languages will be extinct.

In this context, Te Hiku's data and tools represent an alternative epistemic infrastructure, a form of digital decolonization. In a pragmatic sense, the developers see them as "accelerating the revitalization of our language." But in a broader sense, this data insists that their indigenous language—and the concepts, narratives, and worldview embedded within it—are legitimate ways to know. They are not primitive or anachronistic, outdated myths that will slowly fade out until they disappear in the mists of time, but rather vital forms of knowing in the present. "Indigenous languages are not only methods of communication," stresses the UN Forum (2018, 1), "but also extensive and complex systems of knowledge that have developed over millennia." Languages are central to preserving identity and maintaining worldviews. With this in mind, the infrastructuring of a language is a concrete move that fights against the erasure or assimilation of a people and their ways of knowing—an erasure that was seen as "inevitable" at different points in history. From this standpoint, Te Hiku's dataset offers a counter-logic to colonial systems, a reversal of its racialized beliefs.

Far from shunning contemporary information technology, Te Hiku builds on top of it, but does so in a considered way. The group speaks of operating in the "innovation space" and has been one of the first to demonstrate the potential of automatic language recognition for indigenous languages. After receiving a major grant in 2019, the Te Hiku team has hired a number of additional data scientists and Māori language experts. Their work has contributed to developing their data models, model even further, to generating new libraries that they make available on Github, and to collect more spoken audio through their Kōrero Māori mobile app. "We're using technology that, yeah, the colonizers have built," admits Keoni Mahalona (2018), the chief technology officer and a native Hawaiian, "but we're taking that and using that to help accelerate the revitalization of our language."

Te Hiku has gradually refined its automatic speech recognition model, reducing the error rate even further. At the same time, project leaders started presenting their work at conferences, where they received significant interest from other indigenous communities and groups interested in building their own infrastructures. While this interest was welcome, the group also started receiving solicitations from corporations. One corporation based in the United

States started inquiring about the model, and even offered Māori groups $45 US dollars per hour to speak their native language into a telephone so it could be captured. Te Hiku rejected their offer and published a video explaining their decision. "The last thing for the colonizers to take from us is our knowledge and our language and our culture," explained Mahalona (2018), "the things that we keep in here (points to his head) and in our community."

For Te Hiku, the danger is clear. Without maintaining tight control over this data, it will fall into the hands of global corporations whose only interest is economic gain. These companies have no connection to Māori iwi (tribes), and just as importantly, no understanding of its cultural tāonga (treasures). Indeed, the company that approached Te Hiku is creating a global platform for localization by capturing dozens of languages from all over the world. Such data collection lays the groundwork for language-as-a-service, where cloud-based technologies like speech recognition can be rented or subscribed to—for a price. This kind of extraction seems eerily reminiscent of the mechanisms of colonialism, only this time updated with digital tools. In fact, the very idea that knowledge is a thing that can be packaged up, extracted from its roots in a community, and successfully transplanted wherever is a highly Western one. Within the colonial context, knowledge is a kind of raw material, notes Linda Tuhiwai Smith (2021, 188), something just lying there that can be "discovered, extracted, appropriated, and distributed."

Since rejecting that company, Te Hiku has had to fend off approaches from numerous others. Te Hiku's shielding of its data suggests that refusal can be key for alternative infrastructures. To say no, to reject certain values and assumptions, can be an important step for establishing a point of difference and asserting a counter-logic to prevailing norms. In an era when technology companies typically embrace the deep pockets of capital, increased speed, and additional features that major players can provide, this move cuts against the grain. It sets this infrastructure apart as something with different values and vision from its counterparts. Certainly for its developers, improvements to its products and services may be welcome in the future, but these should never come at the expense of the most important feature: self-determination. Better to have an infrastructure that is wholly owned and operated for its people than a system which may be more 'feature-rich' but is run by others. "We don't need anyone else developing the tools which will help us to come to terms with who we are," stated Kathy Irwin (1992, 5), "we can and will do this work. Real power lies with those who design the tools—it always has."

Design-by-removal can also be seen at a granular level. A core part of Te Hiku's work in the last years has been not only to retain the Māori language but also to restore its original sound. The dominance of English over the last 100 years has corrupted the pronunciation of certain words and phrases in Te Reo. The team's new app offers pronunciation guides and strives to remove this influence, "decolonizing the sound of our language." Through their labors, the team carries out a kind of digital excavation, stripping away the impurities that have been attached to its cultural treasures over time. By going back to the past, to older practices, they seek to unearth what was lost and establish more authentic and distinct ways of knowing-and-doing for the future.

For Te Hiku CEO Lucas-Jones (2018), this infrastructure allows Māori people to create their own future and to "facilitate the intergenerational transmission of our culture." Intergenerational transmission kicks against the frenetic timescales that dominate so much contemporary technology and informational infrastructure. An obsession with the new and the next often characterizes these systems. A data center or set of cables is launched for great fanfare. For a brief moment, it is the flagship offering, the infrastructure with the latest specifications sitting at the bleeding edge of technology. However, as we've seen throughout this book, this status fades almost instantly. Within six months, a new site or system comes online, outstripping its rivals and making older incarnations seem outmoded by comparison. In this frenzied context, a product or system has weeks or months to prove itself. If not, it is quickly rendered obsolete. The only thing faster than its rapid rise is its swift decline.

Intergenerational transmission introduces an alternate timescale for infrastructure. The impact of this technical system will not be seen in the next quarterly offering or even the next year, but in 20, 40, or even 100 years' time. This transferral of information from grandmother to mother to granddaughter will take time. It is a process that is fundamentally relational, occurring day after day, season after season, as a child is brought up, discovers the people and things surrounding her, and is taught the words and phrases that correspond to these objects. There is a rhythm to this transmission, a natural cadence to this learning. It cannot be compressed into an electronic packet, shot through a high-wattage cable, and be instantly "captured" on the other side. And partly this is because language is cultural. It is not a matter of simply "downloading" words, but of slowly grasping where those words come from, why they are used, and what they say about a certain people—in short, of understanding an entire life-world. There are rivers and mountains to learn, rituals and customs to internalize, creation myths to grasp that explain the formation of people, the land, the sea, and the sky. This epistemic journey cannot be rushed.

Along with a different timescale, there is a different set of values embedded in this alternative infrastructure. Every way-of-knowing is situated in a particular knowledge tradition which privileges certain values. In the West, these would include a championing of the individual, a stress on "objective" or impartial data, an imperative to classify and codify the world around, and so on. These systems of classification and epistemic frameworks, as Tuhiwai Smith (2021, 145) chronicles, emerge from Enlightenment thought, European philosophy, and colonial history more broadly—they are the world seen through "imperial eyes." The point here is not to condemn the entire knowledge tradition, nor to reify it, but to simply note its specificity. Because it is distinct, it is also inherently limited or even blinkered. In privileging certain ways of knowing, it ignores others.

What would it look like, then, to see the world through other eyes? There are "genuine alternatives," Tuhiwai Smith (2021, 310) reminds us, "starkly contrasting world views" that can generate "starkly different ways of organizing social, political, economic and spiritual life." Alternative infrastructures insist that other ways of knowing exist. Indeed, they point to the fact that dominating epistemologies can often be used to dominate others. Their power consists in defining the frame, defining the values, defining what and who matters. Such hegemonic systems serve to prop up asymmetric power structures and perpetuate inequality. Alternative infrastructures, even those that are transient, improvised, or cobbled together, provide a glimpse of another reality. Through their operations, their performance, they privilege other values. While they're working, we get a fuzzy snapshot of a world that is more local, more communal, more equitable, and more inhabitable—an alternative world.

References

Böhme, Gernot. 2012. *Invasive Technification: Critical Essays in the Philosophy of Technology*. London: Bloomsbury Publishing.
Bryant, Levi. 2014. *Onto-Cartography: An Ontology of Machines and Media*. Edinburgh: Edinburgh University Press.

Coffey, Donavyn. 2021. "Māori Are Trying to Save Their Language from Big Tech." *Wired UK*, April 28, 2021. https://www.wired.co.uk/article/maori-language-tech.

Easterling, Keller. 2016. *Extrastatecraft: The Power of Infrastructure Space*. London: Verso.

Feenberg, Andrew. 2008. *Questioning Technology*. London: Routledge.

Galloway, Alexander R. 2004. *Protocol: How Control Exists after Decentralization*. Cambridge, MA: MIT Press.

Higgins, Rawinia, and Basil Keane. 2015. "Language Decline, 1900 to 1970s." In Te Ara – the Encyclopedia of New Zealand. Ministry for Culture and Heritage Te Manatu Taonga. https://teara.govt.nz/en/te-reo-maori-the-maori-language/page-4.

Irwin, Kathie. 1992. "Towards Theories of Māori Feminism." In *Feminist Voices: Women's Studies Texts for Aotearoa/New Zealand*, edited by Rosemary Du Plessis, 1–22. Oxford: Oxford University Press.

Jünger, Friedrich Georg. 1990. *The Failure of Technology*. Washington, DC: Regnery Gateway.

Lucas-Jones, Peter. 2018. "Indigenous Data Theft." *Te Hiku Media*. August 10, 2018. https://tehiku.nz/p.CFg.

Mahalona, Keoni. 2018. "Indigenous Data Theft." *Te Hiku Media*. August 10, 2018. https://tehiku.nz/p.CFg.

Neilson, Michael. 2020. "Te Wiki o Te Reo Māori: Beaten for Speaking Their Native Tongue, and the Generations That Suffered." *NZ Herald*, September 14, 2020. https://www.nzherald.co.nz/nz/te-wiki-o-te-reo-maori-beaten-for-speaking-their-native-tongue-and-the-generations-that-suffered/F7G6XCM62QAHTYVSRVOCRKAUYI/.

Rogoff, Irit. 2013. "Keynote Lecture: Infrastructure." Presented at the Former West, Berlin, March 20. https://formerwest.org/DocumentsConstellationsProspects/Contributions/Infrastructure.

Smith, Linda Tuhiwai. 2021. *Decolonizing Methodologies: Research and Indigenous Peoples*. London: Zed Books Ltd.

UN Forum on Indigenous Issues. 2018. "Indigenous Languages." April 19, 2018. https://www.un.org/development/desa/indigenouspeoples/wp-content/uploads/sites/19/2018/04/Indigenous-Languages.pdf.

Acknowledgments

This short book was inspired by my work on "Data Centres and the Governance of Labour and Territory," a multi-year research project funded by the Australian Research Council and led by Professor Brett Neilson, Professor Ned Rossiter, and Associate Professor Tanya Notley at the Institute for Culture and Society, Western Sydney University. Thanks to this team for taking me on board and giving me freedom to pursue some interesting and unorthodox lines of enquiry. Thanks also to Professor Harmeet Sawhney, Editor-in-Chief of *The Information Society*, for inviting me to develop this work into a book for the Focus on IT & Society series.

Some of the material here was previously published in academic journals. Chapters 1 and 2 are derived in part from an article published in *New Media and Society*, December 4, 2020, copyright SAGE Publications Ltd, available online: https://doi.org/10.1177/1461444820977197.

Chapter 3 is derived in part from an article published in *Computational Culture*, July 15, 2021, copyright Computational Culture, available online: http://computationalculture.net/imperfect-orchestration-inside-the-data-centers-struggle-for-efficiency/.

And Chapter 4 is derived in part from an article published in *The Information Society*, March 12, 2020, copyright Taylor & Francis, LLC, available online: https://doi.org/10.1080/01972243.2020.1737607.

Greatest thanks of course go to my immediate family Kimberlee, Ari, and Sol, and my extended family, for their work in supporting and sustaining me throughout this research. Your infrastructure of care keeps me going.

Index